W9-BPL-067

BRAVE NEW HOUSES ———

Brave New Houses

ARCHITECTURAL INNOVATION IN SOUTHERN CALIFORNIA

MICHAEL WEBB

Thames & Hudson

Frontispiece: Kanner Architects, Kanner House,
Pacific Palisades. Photograph by Tim Street-Porter.

Any copy of this book issued by the publisher as
a paperback is sold subject to the condition that
it shall not by way of trade or otherwise be lent,
resold, hired out or otherwise circulated without
the publisher's prior consent in any form of binding
or cover other than that in which it is published
and without a similar condition including these
words being imposed on a subsequent purchaser.

First published in the United Kingdom in 2003
by Thames & Hudson Ltd., 181A High Holborn,
London WC1V 7QX

www.thamesandhudson.com

First published in paperback 2005

© 2003 Rizzoli International Publications, Inc.
Text © Michael Webb

All rights reserved. No part of this publication
may be reproduced or transmitted in any form or
by any means, electronic or mechanical, including
photocopy, recording or any other information
storage and retrieval system, without prior
permission in writing from the publisher.

British Library Cataloguing-in-Publication Data
A catalogue record for this book is available from
the British Library

ISBN-13: 978-0-500-28578-7
ISBN-10: 0-500-285578-0

Printed and bound in Hong Kong

OUT OF THE BOX

Southern California was never the Garden of Eden its early boosters promised; rather, it was arid land that could, with effort and irrigation, be made to bloom. That challenge did nothing to diminish its appeal. For over a century, it has lured the struggling and the ambitious from around the world; all of them seeking a fresh start, a new identity, fame, or fortune. Millions more are expected to arrive in the next few decades. The volatile mix of cultures and desires has produced an ephemeral townscape, and a chaotic sprawl of generic dwellings interspersed with vulgar displays of new wealth, but there have always been a few mavericks with the taste and courage to break loose and give talent its chance. Idyllic pockets of wilderness and wooded canyon survive, even at the heart of the metropolis, and still more in the hills around Santa Barbara and San Diego. The coast has been overbuilt, but the ocean retains its pristine appeal. Older neighborhoods have distinct personalities and a few are seeded with modern landmarks. Architects and clients still enjoy unique opportunities to strike out in new directions, uninhibited by tradition and unconstrained by climatic extremes.

Throughout its years of explosive growth, Los Angeles has been a crucible for experimentation in residential design. Irving Gill reinterpreted the Mission style in shallow planes of poured concrete. Frank Lloyd Wright was inspired by Meso-American temples, and sought to create a new American architecture from patterned concrete blocks. Rudolph Schindler and Richard Neutra brought progressive European ideas to a city that was then characterized as Iowa-by-the-Sea, yet found eager clients and built their practices through the Great Depression. In the 1940s, John Entenza launched the Case Study House program, which included steel-frame structures by Charles and Ray Eames, Raphael Soriano, and Pierre Koenig. Gregory Ain and Harwell Hamilton Harris designed frugal dwellings that are treasured today. John Lautner emerged from the shadow of Wright to create soaring structures of wood, concrete, and glass. Frank Gehry launched his career as a "cheapskate architect," infusing simple forms and industrial-grade materials with artistry. Morphosis, Eric Owen Moss, and the late Franklin Israel explored that same gritty aesthetic, using houses as laboratories in which to test their ideas for larger structures.

Successive generations of architects emerged from the offices of these pioneers, to set up their own practices and struggle for recognition. Sadly, a majority of these bold spirits are currently underemployed, and few have made an impact on their community. There's a major disconnect between the potential and the reality of residential design, between the exceptional few and the convention-bound majority.

Most Americans spend too much of their lives in boxes: driving in tin boxes to work, shop, study, or play in larger boxes, before returning home to stucco boxes that are tastefully wrapped in Colonial or Mediterranean-style ornament. Mediterranean living has more to do with sitting under an olive tree, lunching off local produce and a gutsy red wine, breathing in the scents of wild thyme and lavender, than it does with stamped-out moldings, symmetrical doors and windows, and red-tiled roofs. And yet that magic word will sell the trashiest tract house. Retro residences have little to do with the way we dress, move around, and equip ourselves. Nobody goes into a showroom to ask for a Tuscan car or a Cape Cod computer. Equipment is meant to look functional and ahead of the curve; our shelters seem to be caught in a time warp.

Created as status symbols and investments for profitable resale, houses are increasingly shaped by nostalgia for an idealized past and a deep anxiety not to stand out from the crowd. In a nation that prizes freedom and personal expression, conformity rules. Builders dumb down to win acceptance like insecure kids in high school, and neighborhood vigilantes prescribe pitched roofs and an approved color palette in the hope of creating ersatz historic districts. Big is valued far above better, and modern classics are torn down to make room for historical pastiches on steroids that loom menacingly over their neighbors. Once you pass through a columned portico into a lofty foyer with Palladian windows and a crystal chandelier, you may wonder if you've strayed onto the set for a period movie. Where can Miss Scarlett have gone?

A sentimental attachment to an invented past is matched by an instinctive rejection of the unfamiliar. Most Americans now live in suburbs where it's hard to experience the best contemporary architecture first hand—especially on a residential scale. As a result, most people still perceive modernism as cold and unfriendly, and innovative expression as strange and disturbing. Modernism never put down roots in the United States, as it did in Northern Europe, and it enjoyed only the briefest, most superficial acceptance, from about 1925 through 1965. Popular faith in the future shriveled and died in the turbulence of the 1960s. Hollywood established the rules early on: it's the villains who live in sharp houses; good guys slouch around cozy, cluttered homes, coffee mugs in hand, to show that they are just like us.

"Home" is a word that is heavily freighted with emotion—the embodiment of self-image, family, and childhood associations. No wonder so few people can resist its lure. Many of those who would like to break out of the box fear that an architect-designed house may prove too costly or take too long to realize, that the design will be contested or that the end product could prove hard to live with and harder to sell. Their home may be their only substantial asset and they are afraid to put it at risk.

Gathered here are thirty-four houses commissioned by people who were willing to take a chance and please themselves. Old and young, affluent or with limited means, connoisseurs and neophytes, these clients are as diverse as their dwellings. Each individual, couple, or family wanted something tailored to their dreams and practical needs, to the site and the climate, and all found architects who would listen and respond, creating houses that fulfilled their program and brought boundless rewards. In a few cases, the architect was also the client. Without exception, they found that their lives as well as their portfolios were enriched. Formerly skeptical friends congratulated them on their good fortune. Strangers came on tours and envied what they saw. Delays or cost overruns during construction were quickly forgotten.

None of this happened by chance. Designing a house is a balancing act—satisfying present and future requirements while addressing the site and context and giving the architect abundant scope for creativity. Success depends as much on careful planning as flights of inspiration. It is crucial to choose your architect with as much care as you select your life partner—the relationship can bring a couple together or cause a

split, and it can last even longer. Almost as crucial is the selection of a contractor. Make a list of what you want and of houses and features you like, in photographs or real life. Conduct interviews, make field visits, and talk to owners about their experience. The firm you select may have a signature or change its style with every job; it may be headed by a veteran or a fledgling architect. That's less important than getting the full attention of the individual who will be making the key decisions. The best buildings are the product of chemistry: the client talking and analyzing, the architect listening and explaining, sketching, modeling, and sharing a vision. Good clients know when to talk back and demand alternatives, and when to stay silent and participate in a journey to a place they've never been before and may not have imagined.

This is a personal selection of new and recent houses, located from Santa Barbara to San Diego counties, but mostly in greater LA. What unites this region is its Mediterranean climate: generally sunny and dry, with warm days and cool nights, and increasingly temperate as you move higher or approach the ocean. You can live outdoors for much of the year: something that astounds visitors, though residents often take it for granted. The house that Schindler built for himself in West Hollywood, eighty years ago, was inspired by a camping trip and remains a model of indoor-outdoor living. Nearly all the houses shown here are inspired by that idea and are designed to be naturally cooled, through cross ventilation, and warmed by passive solar gain in winter.

Each house occupies one of six thematic groups (three form-driven, three identified by site) but might feel just as much at home in another. The goal is less to categorize than to explore affinities, while examining radically different approaches to design in a wide range of sizes, situations, and budgets. These houses were chosen because they satisfy needs and address their sites in an elegant and/or inventive way. They are all modern in spirit, drawing on the enduring lessons of the past without mimicking its outward forms. Many are remodels, the new conducting a dialogue with the old, or merely taking advantage of existing footprints to avert a tedious quest for new building permits.

The first section, *Shifting Geometries*, shows how you can achieve complexity by sliding and rotating boxy volumes, as Stan Allen did in Glendale, or by employing Patrick Tighe's strategy of dividing a rectangular volume with a diagonal wall to create a house that doubles as an art gallery in West Hollywood. In *Serene Volumes*, Holger Schubert's canalside house is only a seventh the size of Charles Gwathmey's hilltop palazzo, but both are spas for the spirit, places in which your pulse rate slows as you step inside. *Dynamic Structures* covers more ground. In the windswept Tejon Pass, Michael Jantzen turned cement board and steel frames into habitable origami, and RoTo Architects created a loft from salvaged steel on an industrial site in downtown LA.

Fronting the Ocean includes a house by Ray Kappe in Malibu that feels as though it is surfing, and another, by Callas Shortridge in Castellammare, which floats high above the Pacific. *Engaging the Landscape* is an elastic term that could apply to many of the houses in the book, but these five open up to nature and draw it inside. Barton Myers performed this feat on a heroic scale in the hills of Montecito, while Melinda Gray established an intimate relationship with the wooded slopes of Rustic Canyon. *Confined Lots* is likely to prove a growth area, as scarce land escalates in price. Architecture flourishes on constraints, and Whitney Sander responded to the challenge of a tiny, hemmed-in plot on a Venice canal, as Lorcan O'Herlihy did on a precipitous site in Silver Lake.

A seventh section, *Radical Visions*, anticipates the creativity we can look forward to if even more people decide to think out of the box. One of these houses is under construction, three are in design development, and the last is the product of speculation.

SHIFTING GEOMETRIES

Static forms become kinetic when you rotate one against another, play curved walls off straight, or taper a room to force the perspective. The six houses described here employ these and similar strategies to relate the building to an irregular site, to layer and enrich simple volumes, make interiors seem larger than they are, and achieve a sense of surprise.

1

Linda Burnham's house is a silvery, cubist composition that faces onto a quiet residential street and backs onto a busy underpass, vistas of warehouses, palm trees, and a backdrop of mountains: a quintessential LA setting that could be replicated all over the city. An artist and professor at the Otis Art Institute, she had shared a live-work space with her late husband, the painter Robert Overby, but found the converted warehouse was uncomfortably large to live in by herself. A friend introduced her to Stan Allen, currently Dean of the Princeton School of Architecture, at the 1996 Pritzker Prize ceremony for Rafael Moneo in the unfinished Getty Center. Burnham admired Allen's New York art galleries and, though he was based there and had yet to design a ground-up structure, she

invited him over to her studio. "There were books on Eileen Gray, Mies, and Rem Koolhaas on her table, so I thought I was in the right place," the architect recalls. "Our sensibilities meshed and she proved to be an ideal client, giving me a very open program and then joining in an extended dialogue, face-to-face and by fax."

Though Burnham's basic requirements were simple—lots of light, open, flexible rooms, and a nice bathroom—she had strong ideas about how she wanted the spaces to work, how they would be connected, and how the light would be modulated. Allen had spent two years with Moneo in Spain and understood how to control harsh sunlight, and he had learned from his six galleries that "you should notice the art before the architecture. In a domestic

situation the architecture can be a little more forward," he observes, "but it should serve as a frame and a backdrop to the life of the house, rather than dominate and control it."

Though architect and client were on the same page, there were many unforeseen delays. The site was zoned commercial, the boundary line between the studio and a church ran through the footprint, and the east and west sides were both considered as frontages, requiring setbacks. Putting a pool in the backyard required a separate application. Securing waivers took two years, but it allowed the design to evolve. "Our first scheme was generated in plan," says Allen. "When we took it up again, we began with the section, and then went back to the plan to establish lines of sight from one room to another and

1 The master bathroom projects out over the pool to the rear
2 First and second floor plans

Plans throughout the book have been annotated using the following key
B bedroom
D dining
E entry
G garage
GYM exercise room
K kitchen
L living
MB master bedroom
MR media room, den
P pool
S study, studio, library
T terrace, deck, balcony
VD void to area below

2

out to the street on which the house is aligned." Finally, they had to win approval from the city authorities at a publicly televised design hearing. They were full of apprehension, since Glendale has few good modern buildings; however, by presenting a balsa-wood model and a tan-painted sample of the aluminum cladding, they breezed through.

It was worth the wait. Boxy elements clad in brushed aluminum that reflects the color of the sky rotate and jut, imparting a sense of motion and lightness. The garage and guest room push out to the east and north, and the upstairs master bathroom slides out like a drawer to the west. The garage, which flanks the entry, is a translucent volume with corrugated fiberglass sides and a mesh roll-up door. A gray-tinted stucco

plane with an oval cutout extends over the upstairs deck, and the opening is echoed in the entrance canopy and skylights. Allen says he was tipping his hat to Aalto, but there may be an unconscious reference to Albert Frey's first space-age house in Palm Springs. The ribbed aluminum is pulled inside to clad a curved wall that divides the double-height living room from the master bedroom. The open-sided kitchen with its thick ply counter is tucked in below, providing a pleasing shift from lofty to intimate ceiling heights. A tightly coiled stair leads up to the office, the bedroom with its tilted ceiling, and a spacious mosaic-lined bathroom with a sweeping view to the mountains.

The 2,300-square-foot house is a constant source of delight for its owner. Though the plan is lucid, there's an

intricacy that comes from a collaboration in which every facet of the design was thought through and resolved. The contractor, Group F, showed unusual dedication in getting the details right, and Pamela Burton did the landscaping. For Allen, it was a learning experience. "Working in Southern California makes you part of a very strong tradition— I felt that Schindler and Neutra were looking over my shoulder," he says. "For me, West Coast architects are more hands-on and experimental than they are back East; the attitude is, try something and see if it will work."

3 Translucent garage juts at an angle to the rectilinear house
4 Stucco plane with an oval cutout over the second-floor deck

5 Looking down to the dining area
from the mezzanine gallery
6 The dining area opens up
through sliders to garden and pool
7 Looking over the living area to
the kitchen and entry

On a quiet Beverly Hills street lined with traditional cottages, the Weissberg house pulls off the tricky feat of standing out and fitting in. It's a symphony of curves. Crisp white walls billow out to the street corner, and a gray metal roof arches over the living areas and down to respect the scale of the neighbors. Unshaded windows are placed high up to protect the owners' privacy yet offer tantalizing glimpses of the spaces behind the walls, and the expanses of stucco are relieved by the spiky plantings of LA landscape designer Judy Farber.

After spending half their lives in an aging house nearby, the Weissbergs decided it was time for a fresh start. Initially, the wife was reluctant to commission a ground-up house, but she changed her mind after seeing the new offices of Acorn Paper, her husband's packaging firm. The architect, Hagy Belzberg, had worked with Frank Gehry on the design of the Bilbao Guggenheim before setting up his own office, where he began to specialize in houses and restaurants. Convinced they had found the right designer, the Weissbergs abandoned their search for a condo and went looking for a teardown.

The lot they eventually found was zoned for up to 4,600 square feet of enclosed space, but they decided they could have all the room they needed and a more graceful profile with only 3,600. They asked Belzberg to put the master suite on the ground floor and avoid a boxy look. "I like curves," says Mrs. Weissberg, "and that's what I got. During construction, neighbors would call up and say, 'Are you aware that the beams aren't straight?'" She knew very well because she was on site every day. "Each step was exciting," she recalls, "and it took only fourteen months from groundbreaking to the day we moved in." The contractor, Group F, did an exemplary job of construction.

Belzberg created three zones. Bordering the street to the north is the master suite, its bathroom opening onto a walled patio and a jet resistance pool. Garage, kitchen and eating areas are ranged along the south side, with a guest bedroom, an office, and a gym upstairs. Sandwiched between is the gracefully curved living room. This extends from the study inside the rounded stucco prow beside the entry, back to the garden. On plan, these sections are as tightly locked together as the pieces of a jigsaw puzzle, and the lazy "S" of

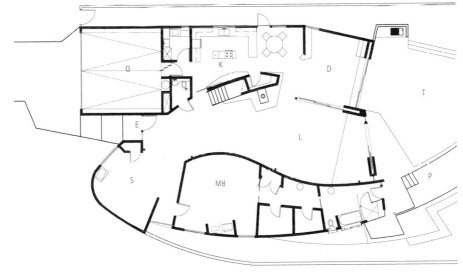

1 Arched roof and curved walls scale the house to its neighbors
2 First floor plan

2

the wall that divides living from sleeping areas gives a distinctive character to both.

From the low portal of the entrance, you step into the soaring, light-filled living room, which is lit from windows at either end and from the ellipse of glass beneath the arched ceiling vault. This clerestory frames a strip of sky and the branches of a magnolia, and the double-glazing shuts out the sounds of traffic. Upstairs rooms are expressed as angles jutting through the wall, complementing the sculptural hearth. The dining area can be treated as an open space linking the kitchen/breakfast area and garden terrace to the living room. Alternatively, for formal entertaining or to achieve a greater sense of intimacy, it can be enclosed by sliding, wood-framed panels of sand-blasted glass that resemble Japanese shoji screens.

Interior designer Milo Baglioni has collaborated with Belzberg on three of his houses, and was associated with this project from the beginning. "For the Weissbergs, the priorities were music and art," he explains, "and that shaped everything I did. The piano is her most precious possession, and she wanted a place where she could play and share her pleasure with guests, besides doing a lot of entertaining." He designed comfortable chairs and sofas to complement a few pieces the clients brought with them, and grouped these around the piano and hearth. A sophisticated speaker system carries music to every part of the house.

Belzberg and Baglioni chose a muted palette to set off the Weissbergs' art collection, which includes boldly colored paintings by Roy Lichtenstein and Sam Francis, as well as subtle works on paper. Maple is used throughout—straight-grain on the floor and birdseye for the built-in cabinets, with bleached ash in the kitchen. Putty and beige walls and fabrics, including an area rug that suggests raked sand, are enlivened with soft tones of blue and green. This is a house in which the decor subtly enhances the architecture, adding warmth and refinement without compromising its sweep.

3 An undulating wall divides the living area from the master suite
4 Second floor plan
5 (overleaf) Layered walls and high openings ensure privacy from the street

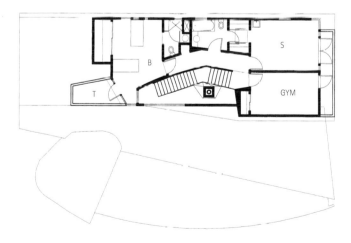

4

6 Double-glazed clerestories shut
out noise and provide natural light
7 The dining room and kitchen can
be enclosed with sliding screens
8 Looking from the dining room to
the piano in the living area

Many of the houses in this collection are technically remodels, employing the foundations and fragments of the old as the point of departure for a new invention. The Wing house is more like a second act. Wallace Cunningham radically reshaped his first house, completed in 1981, for a new owner who encouraged him to expand and refine his original design. The process stretched over three years—much longer than it took to build from scratch the first time around. The roof was raised six inches, the bedroom wing was extended, every surface was changed. Only the plan remained essentially unaltered: two semicircular arcs intersecting to enclose an elliptical living area and a paved courtyard with a new crescent-shaped pool. The contractor was Chuck Lang Construction.

Ironically, the clients who bought the only modern house in this resolutely retro community and insisted on a rigorous minimalism had raised their family in a six-bedroom Tudor-style house on Lake Michigan. Now the couple felt it was time for a fresh start in a compact house that opened up to a hillside and took full advantage of a benign climate. Cunningham responded to the challenge. Self-taught (but for six months at Taliesin) he has swum far out of the mainstream, becoming a natural successor to John Lautner in his mastery of curved and angular geometries and the fertility of his invention. Both architects refused to compromise, and suffered rejection by editors seeking the newest celebrity or trend.

It's a tribute to Cunningham's persistence that the original house got built. The design review board wanted to reject it outright, even though it was located on a four-acre site and was impossible to see from the road. "We slowly wore them down," says the architect with a smile.

You wonder why anyone should have objected to a house that, for all its originality, hugs the slope and offers so unthreatening a facade. The knife-edge roof conceals its steel frame beneath a gently pitched expanse of standing seam copper. The concrete block walls, refaced in creamy toned, steel-troweled stucco, shimmer in light reflected from the pool and alternate with expanses of curved and mitered glass. French limestone pavers, laid in a herringbone pattern, flow through the glass to link interiors and terraces. Beyond the house, granite treads

1 Looking down on the curved wall planes from the upper garden
2 First floor plan

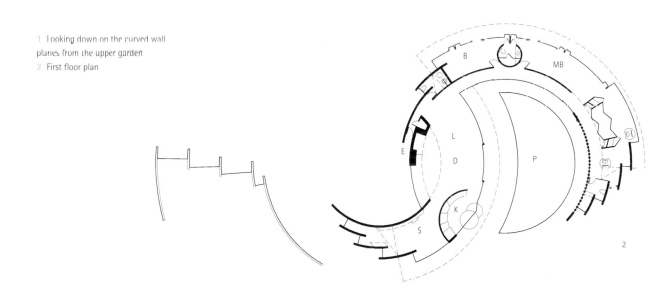

ascend to a Jacuzzi that provides an ideal vantage point from which to look down on the house and appreciate the layering of curvilinear walls that wrap around each other as snugly as the rings in a tree trunk.

A path curves up from the garage, buried in the hillside, to the pool terrace. You can enter through the compact kitchen with its curved and stepped cherry-wood cabinets, which is screened from the dining area by a curved wall that stops short of the gently pitched ceiling. A library curves back towards the front of the house, and a guest bedroom is tucked in below. The expansive living room is lit from sliders that open to the pool and an elliptical skylight that cuts across the entrance facade. The furnishings are simple, but for a sculptural de Sede sofa, and the materials are consistent throughout.

The second arc of the house contains a powder room that is doubled in size by a mirrored back wall, another guest bedroom, and the master suite. The bedrooms face out to the hillside, and are dappled by squares of light from the pierced openings in the wall bordering the pool. The dressing area has concertina folded doors of translucent glass supported on steel poles that are lit from within by fluorescent tubes. Beyond are black granite basins with pivoting cabinets below.

The owners are pleased to discover that the 3,850-square-foot house is energy self-sufficient. There is cross ventilation in every room, and a steady ocean breeze up the canyon so they have yet to use the air-conditioning.

The thermal mass holds heat from the low sun and the house required heating for only three days last winter. Natural lighting is well balanced and is mimicked by concealed tungsten lighting.

Cunningham considers this job "the most rewarding I've ever done— to make the place get up and sing. The original idea was good, but the finishes and details have achieved an entirely new level of excellence. I reduced all the elements to return to the concept of roofs floating over radiating walls. Best of all, we got to design everything, from hinges and cabinets to rugs; there's almost nothing off the shelf."

3 Kitchen with stepped cabinets and counters penetrating glass
4 Elliptical living room, skylight, and screen wall around kitchen
5 (overleaf) Pierced openings in the bedroom wing are reflected in the pool

6 The translucent glass closet doors resemble a folding screen

7 Angled glass doors complement the sensuously curved wall

8 Black granite pedestals reflected in the mirrored powder room

9 Master bathroom cabinet with curved, swing-out drawers

10 The play of light through openings in the master bedroom

Live-work spaces are increasingly common, but few integrate two functions as successfully as the house-gallery that Patrick Tighe designed for Michael Collins and his Art Form Gallery on a leafy residential street. The challenge was to create, within the footprint of a 1,400-square-foot bungalow, expansive and intimate spaces for the display of emerging LA artists' work, shown by appointment, as well as a stylish living-entertaining environment. Collins admired the angular underground gallery that Tighe, a former associate of Thom Mayne at Morphosis, had added to the Jacobs house in the San Fernando Valley and commissioned the newly independent architect to remodel the house he had bought for its proximity to the galleries of West Hollywood. "I gave him carte blanche,"

says Collins, "asking for as much hanging space as possible with state-of-art lighting, two bedrooms, two baths, and an office."

To avoid tough new zoning restrictions, Tighe retained fifty percent of the existing perimeter, but was allowed to raise the roof. His big move was to divide the interior diagonally with a new load-bearing wall that defines a long open wedge of living-display space and a succession of private rooms behind. A new roof tilts up from the old east wall to frame a clerestory over the diagonal wall and extends to shade this slot from direct sun. The duality of the interior is expressed in the street facade with its translucent storefront glazing to the left of the entry and a corner window carved out of a projecting bay to the right. The house is a work of art

in itself, clad in zinc scales and sharply distinct from its Mediterranean-style stucco neighbors, yet similar in size. It feels private and expansive, even though the building and a detached garage-studio to the rear occupy much of the 4,000-square-foot lot.

A five-foot-wide pivoting glass door creates an impressive threshold and connects the house visually to the street and the distant hills. As you step inside, the forced perspective of the tapered plan and a black, steel reflecting pool in the rear patio make the space feel much longer than it is. The clerestory is the principal source of natural light, eliminating the need for windows down the side walls, thus maximizing display space. There's an aluminum rail from which pictures can be suspended on cables and a cantilevered steel

1 The art gallery and guest bedroom are expressed in the facade
2 First floor plan

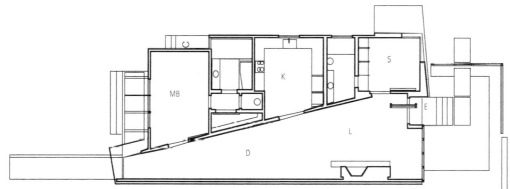

2

3 To the rear, a raised pool reflects
extended axis of the gallery
4 The intimate master bedroom
opens onto a shaded rear deck

armature for track lighting, which can be dimmed to achieve ambient illumination. When a large exhibition opens, every part of the house is put to use. Paintings can be displayed on the white stucco hood of the fireplace, which juts out at a right angle to the tilted roof, in the bedrooms, and even on the steel-troweled plaster wall of the shower.

Barcelona chairs and a day bed are grouped around the hearth at the front of the gallery, and Tighe designed the tapered steel-framed dining table. Sliding doors of opaque laminated glass separate the gallery from the guest bedroom and bathroom in front, the central kitchen with its stainless counter mounted on casters, and the master suite to the rear. The art gains from being shown in a residential setting, which, for neophyte collectors,

is less intimidating than a commercial gallery. Collins and his partner get to live with the art he has collected, and he feels that he has achieved the best of both worlds under one roof. "The lighting is as good here as in the best museums," he says. "The natural light from the clerestory to the west is perfect, and the track lighting is color-corrected to simulate daylight. The hanging system is quick and easy to use, and it spares the walls." He also praises the skill of contractor Karl Tso.

The paved patio to the south is an outdoor room that works well for receptions and relaxation. The tall window of the gallery is mirrored in the pool, and its vertical thrust plays off the horizontal bay of the master bedroom, with its steel-troweled wall of soft gray stucco and its glass doors

opening onto a terrace that is shaded by a projecting steel grille. Bamboo screens out the neighbors, and Collins's office is located in the garage, which has been upgraded with redwood siding, a large sliding glass door, and a skylight. Tighe has created a succession of refined spaces that work well for the art and the occupants, energizing them with the dynamic play of geometry he absorbed at Morphosis, but giving them his own distinctive stamp.

5 Looking from the living area to
the tapered end of the gallery
6 Tighe designed the steel-framed
dining table to echo the plan
7 The hearth is a place to view art
and a focus for living

1

An almost unbroken expanse of beige stucco—more wall than facade—conceals the Weil house from the street and its modestly scaled neighbors. Only the circle of succulents and bright green mosses in the front yard draws attention. Look closer, and you'll see a hint of what lies beyond: a beveled plane that juts out over the walls and protects the recessed entry. Step inside and you are drawn forward by watery reflections dancing on a long tapering soffit that flies across a lap pool, leading your gaze to the end of a triangular living area that's as open and transparent as the front is closed. It's a wonderfully theatrical gesture, like a curtain rising on a brightly lit stage.

Leslie Weil is a writer, and her husband, Scott, does voice-overs and photography. They spend much of their time working at home and were planning to start a family, so they went searching for a house with free-flowing space, great light, a rational layout, warmth and beauty. The enclave of late-1940s houses by Gregory Ain in Mar Vista convinced them of the virtues of modernism, but the prices of those classics have soared, and they settled for a modest, yellow stucco bungalow close by. It had few of the qualities they were seeking, but it did have a good location and an expansive trapezoidal site. Their neighbor's children played with those of an architect, and this casual recommendation brought them to the office of Godfredsen Sigal, who showed them a house they had built in the Hollywood Hills. The Weils commissioned a modest remodel, which turned into something more ambitious.

Ron Godfredsen and Danna Sigal were near-contemporaries at UCLA and Yale who married and established a versatile partnership in 1994. They gutted the existing house, saving only two bedrooms, removed the roof, and reconfigured the living area as a new master suite that opens onto a Zen-like gravel courtyard with a dwarf blue cedar behind the front wall. A charcoal soapstone tub projects through the glass into the court to create the illusion that you are bathing outdoors. The master bedroom and a family room open up to a patio and look out to the garage, which has been turned into a skylit studio. The tapered entry foyer serves as a hinge between old and new and leads into the living area, which is bounded by two walls of glass and one that is lined with custom cabinets

1 The wedge-shaped living room opens onto the pool and deck
2 First floor plan

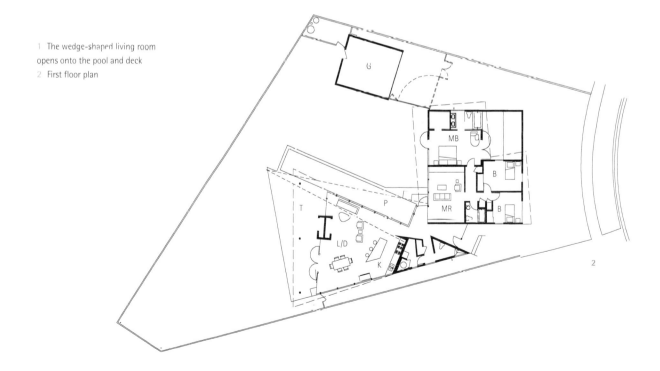

concealing the kitchen appliances and supplies, while blocking the westerly sun. A two-way fireplace is set into the glass of the end wall and the roof extends over a patio that is treated as an outdoor living room with Philippe Starck's plastic club chairs drawn up to the hearth. The kitchen counter, dining table, and sitting areas form islands on the polished concrete floor. Scott Weil had dreamed of transporting a Soho loft to LA and walking out into the sunshine, and his wife wanted to join the party rather than being exiled to a closed-off kitchen. Both got their wish.

The house has grown from 1,100 to 2,500 square feet of enclosed space, but it feels far more expansive. The pool is reflected in the glass so that it appears from the outside to be flowing across the floor. The tapered soffit tilts gently down and reflects light onto the ceiling canopy, which is tilted up and supported on slender steel columns. The sharp angles of the two planes play off each other and the rectilinearity of the old, turning the structure into a kinetic sculpture that shifts as you move around it. The entire house is dematerialized by the play of light and reflections.

"We wanted to layer the space and create places your eyes can walk to even if your feet can't," says Sigal. "Wherever you stand, you are looking across the pool to another part of the house and often into it." Doors and windows open to provide cross ventilation and the concrete floor absorbs the winter sun. The clients wanted a house that was warm as well as modern, and the architects satisfied that need with the impeccably crafted cabinets and joinery of straight-grain Douglas fir, and subtle shifts of color from one room to the next. The windows frame the drought-resistant, dog-tolerant "meadow" of carex grasses, which offer another layer of color and texture. The architects designed the triangular stainless sink in the powder room and hired Doug Dalton, a longtime collaborator, as contractor.

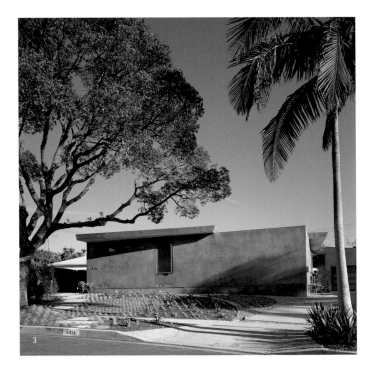

3 New roofs peeking over the blank facade of the old house
4 Kitchen cabinets block westerly sun from the living area

4

5 Reflections from the pool playing
across the tapered soffit
6 Looking from the living area to
the entrance and kitchen

Richard and Vickie Blades lost their ranch house and everything they owned in a brush fire that devastated the wooded canyons to the west of Santa Barbara in June 1990. While their neighbors were quickly rebuilding in the image of the past, this couple was determined to make a fresh start. The site was free of design restrictions and they could build whatever they pleased. "The idea was to put something new into the world, just as we had done in designing computer software, and as I always tried to do as an artist," says Richard. They failed to find a local architect who shared their vision of a house with concrete walls and a muscular steel structure, lofty volumes, and huge openings in place of conventional doors and windows. Instead, they turned to Thom Mayne, the principal of an LA firm he co-founded with Michael Rotondi in 1979. It had won awards for daring projects but had yet to secure the large-scale international commissions that now sustain it. Thus began a five-year saga of design and construction that would bring exhilaration and moments of despondency, and cost the clients every dollar they had or could borrow.

Mayne, and project architects Mark McVay and Kim Groves, listened to the Blades, and developed a first model that incorporated all the key features of the final design: a linear sequence of open spaces, stepping up the slope from south to north, with a bowed ceiling arching up from the kitchen, over the living areas, and down again to embrace the master bedroom. Glass sliders to either side link these spaces to outdoor rooms within the sweep of a curved concrete wall that is cut away where it penetrates the house and bridges the lap pool. A sculpture studio that was part of the original plan is now being built to the east of the entry; stairs lead up to Vickie's office, which projects out through a curved roof that is armored with standing-seam bonderized metal.

The model was fine-tuned and tweaked for almost a year. As Richard recalls: "We refined the plan to make the house more habitable, changing proportions and relationships between the parts, and questioning everything the architects proposed until Thom said, 'Can't you simply trust me?' He told us they worked harder on this project than anything else they'd done before, and I can believe it."

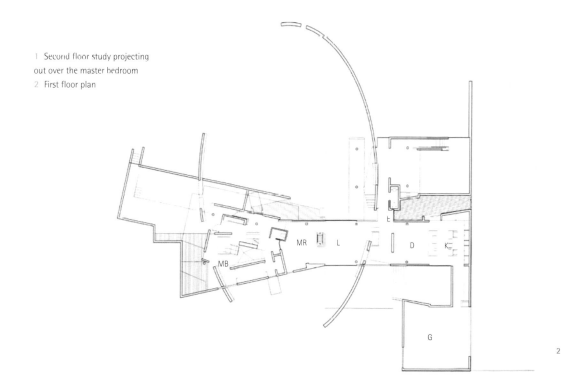

1 Second floor study projecting out over the master bedroom
2 First floor plan

The contractor was the third essential player. Kirk Lewis (of Froscher-Lewis Design and Construction) had a college degree, made furniture in his spare time, and was married to an architect. He guessed the job would take about twelve months, but that proved much too optimistic. At the end of the first year, they had a foundation, a structural frame, and impeccably poured concrete walls. The house took nearly three more years to complete—perhaps inevitably, since this is a one-of-a-kind. Client and contractor solved problems on site. To clear-coat the dakua plywood lining of the vault, eight applications were required, and the final layers had to be hand-brushed. The steel columns arrived half-rusted and were wire-brushed and sealed to achieve a richly textured look that requires no mainte-

nance. Morphosis specified corrugated eterboard—a thin concrete panel—to provide fire-retardant exterior cladding. The Blades disliked its looks and discovered it might crack and would need to be painted. Instead, the entrance facade is faced with redwood battens concealing panels that are tightly sealed to meet the fire code.

The Blades have now lived in the house for six years and it has turned out to be as stimulating and satisfying as they had hoped. Tough yet sensual, firmly rooted but airborne, it soars and embraces its occupants, and it blurs the division between indoors and out. It encloses spaces that are alternately grand and intimate, which extend through subtly layered outdoor areas to draw in the landscape. Sunlight models the forms and textures of the

house and, on moonlit nights, Richard walks through the house to experience the play of shadows through the openings that are carved out of the shell. There are no doors, even around the sunken shower and the bedroom that opens onto the pool. The pulleys that lift the fire doors on the central hearth are sculptural objects, as are the pipe-rail balustrades the owners crafted, yet there is a simple honesty in the way natural materials are expressed. The concrete floor absorbs the winter sun and is radiantly heated; cross ventilation keeps the interior cool in summer.

3 Plywood-lined ceiling vault arches down over the kitchen
4 Poured concrete wall is cut away to frame the living area

5 Redwood battens flank the narrow recess leading to entry
6 Steel-railed balcony juts like a springboard over the pool
7 The house resembles a massive sculpture in the landscape

SERENE VOLUMES

The great luxuries in residential architecture are space and light, and the two are interconnected. Rooms that are tall enough to pull in the sky and staircases that seem to ascend to heaven lift our spirits. These four houses range in size from grand to modest, but each offers an alternation of intimate and expansive volumes, solid and void, enclosure and release.

Over the past thirty-five years, Charles Gwathmey has created a succession of grandly proportioned and meticulously ordered residences that embody the spirit of modernism. The house he recently completed for a professional couple and their four children in the Santa Monica Mountains has that same purity of form, but it is infused by a sensuality and intimacy that are new to his work—a spirit that reflects the desires of the clients and the drama of the site.

It grows from a promontory that juts out to the south and west. You approach diagonally from the north, catching a distant glimpse of the ocean while descending sixty feet to the motor court. From here, the house is like a wall, holding back the view, except for the glass-sided dining room, which frames the skyline and seems

to float on a reflecting pool. Gwathmey speaks of carving away a solid mass to articulate each part of the house, reduce its bulk, and open it up to the landscape. Curved walls play off sheer planes, an inverted cone (supporting a third-floor Jacuzzi that is accessed from the master bedroom) complements the living room rotunda. Like a sculpture that yields fresh discoveries as you move around it, the house is constantly evolving; a gleaming multifaceted object animated by the play of shadow and watery reflections. So carefully scaled and proportioned is the building that it's hard to guess it contains 20,000 square feet of enclosed space on the three floors and basement, and in the sauna–guest house on the far side of the pool. The contractor was Ardie Tavangarian of the ARYA Group.

The sculptural richness of the exterior is carried inside, but the first and most lasting impression is one of serenity. Louis Kahn used mass to instill a feeling of quietness in his buildings; Gwathmey employs interlocking, light-filled volumes to achieve the same calming effect. Bold axes guide you eastward from the entry through the dining room to the kitchen and family room, or south to the living areas, but the axes rotate subtly to impart a sense of movement. The patterns of circulation and the lighting are calculated to draw you through the house, as smoothly as a fish swimming through water. Orthogonal and curvilinear geometries are overlaid, as in the living room, where the square master bedroom seems to be suspended within the rotunda. The circle is completed

1 Pool, north-east facades and entry court from guest house
2 First floor plan

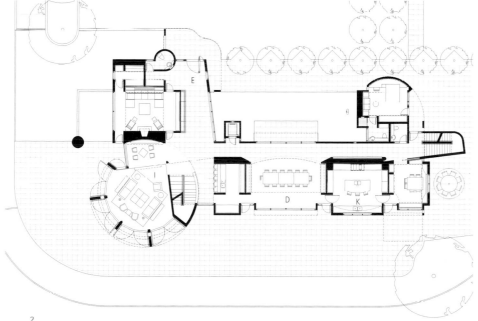

2

around the staircase, which appears to be carved from a solid block of white stucco. A curved soffit and maple-strip floor arcing out into the granite-paved concourse define the dining area.

The owners insisted on rooms that would nurture family life as well as spaces for entertaining close friends or a crowd. Gwathmey, and associate partner Gerald Gendreau, gave them a hierarchy of spaces, ranging from the lofty living room to a low-ceilinged library and a three-story stair hall. The dining table seats twelve, but ten times as many can spill out through sliders to front and back terraces, using the table as a buffet. Every space has been carefully planned and proportioned to satisfy practical and emotional needs. The consistent rhythm of glazing bars provide a frame for the play of light,

and the two combine in reflections off the shallow moat which wraps around the living spaces. A few high-grade materials, impeccably detailed and finished, are used throughout, and built-in cabinetry complements an elegant mix of one-off and classic modern furnishings.

The staircase has a fluidity that recalls the best of Alvar Aalto, and these lyrical forms are carried through the second-floor work areas. The secretary's desk winds sinuously around a corner of the stair landing and leads back to the wife's office with its wave-form shelves and a spiral stair leading up to her bathroom. A pyramidal ceiling vault with cove lighting turns the master bedroom into a pavilion that seems to hover above the city; the architect calls it his reinterpretation of the traditional

attic. There is a basement theater that doubles as a cozy retreat for informal entertaining, and the owners brought in a team of Finnish craftsmen to build a traditional sauna (to remind the wife of her native land) in the detached guest house.

Gwathmey praises the clients for their intense involvement over the seven years of design and construction. "They were incredibly energetic and curious," he recalls, "and that intensity compelled me to recognize and resolve every facet of the design. We always try to engage clients in a dialogue and a collaboration, but their commitment is a huge leap of faith. No matter how many models and computer renderings we make, few people understand the complexity of the spaces before they are built."

3 Foyer leading into rotunda (left) and intimate sitting area
4 Entrance and cone reaching up to the master bedroom level

4

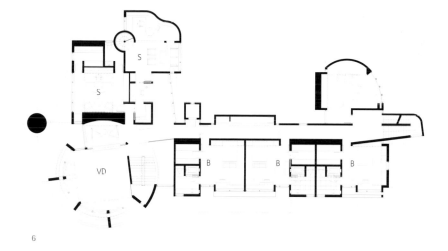

6

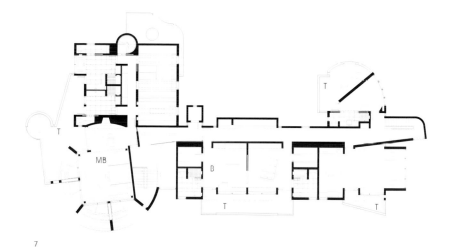

5 The living room rotunda is the symbolic hub of the house
6 Second floor plan
7 Third floor plan

7

8 Intimate sitting area washed
in light reflected from pool
9 Second floor landing leading
to studies and children's bedrooms
10 Sliders open the dining room
to a moat and the city lights

11

11 An ellipse in the floor and the soffit defines the dining room
12 Organic cabinetry and a spiral stair in the wife's office
13 The lofty rotunda embraces the landscape and the sky
14 The master bedroom feels as though it is floating in midair

1

Michael Palladino is a design partner with Richard Meier & Partners, who moved from New York to open the LA office soon after the firm won the 1984 competition to design the Getty Center, and stayed on after its completion. He and Meier speak the same classic modern language, but with a different intonation, and Palladino's recent addition to a 1954 bungalow has a more relaxed quality than one might expect from this rigorous office.

It was undertaken for Gil Friesen, an art-loving entrepreneur who was president of a record company and has since embarked on a new business career. "Usually we won't take on remodels—it's so time-consuming you can lose your shirt," says Palladino, "but Gil is an old friend and has a beautiful property." Marc Peter, Jr, a Swiss-born businessman who studied architecture at Harvard, built the original house for his family in 1953, with the help of another immigrant, the Dutch-born architect Joseph van der Kar. Friesen bought this modern classic for its good bones and indoor-outdoor quality, and he invited Pamela Burton to landscape the hillside as a setting for his fine collection of contemporary sculpture.

Palladino had earlier stripped unsympathetic additions and enlarged the living room by wrapping glass around a twelve-foot-wide rear terrace. Now, working with project architect Michael Gruber, he added a second story comprising a library and study at either end of the L-plan, and a spacious master suite between, increasing the size of the house to 8,600 square feet. The first floor was to be reconfigured as public space, plus a guest bedroom. Architect and client wanted to stay within the footprint of the old house, respect its proportions and save the existing walls, while centering the rambling plan, opening it to the sky, and establishing a stronger connection to the garden.

The second story was built on a platform supported by three parallel shear walls that provide seismic bracing for the entire structure. From the entrance court and the terrace overlooking the garden, you would suppose this to be a ground-up house, so seamless is the junction of old and new. Though much of the existing fabric and its windows have been retained, your eye is drawn to the curved screen walls that cut into the front and mask the study over the garage, and the

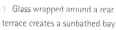

1 Glass wrapped around a rear terrace creates a sunbathed bay
2 First floor plan

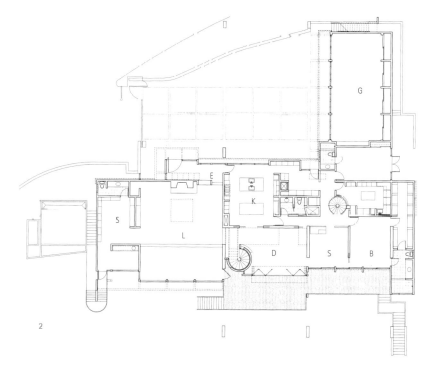

2

cutaway shear walls that project like outriggers from the facade. A top-lit spiral stair acts a centering device for the garden side. The white stucco skin is complemented by painted aluminum plates cladding the curvilinear elements. Translucent glass in the first floor facade and garage doors imparts a sense of mystery and the house glows like a lantern at night.

The crisp geometry of the facades is a foil to the mature trees that dominate the site, reaching out almost to touch them and draw them metaphorically into the house. But the architect's productive collaboration with his client is best demonstrated by the interior, in which a few dramatic moves are complemented by a wealth of subtle detail. Tom Farrage fabricated the painted steel spiral stair, as tightly coiled as a

spring, leading up to the second-floor deck, which is shaded by a painted steel trellis. Natural light floods down to the living room through the skylit open space between terrace and library, and throughout the house from clerestories and precisely placed slots. Walls and floors are gently washed with light, but the intensity is carefully regulated by *brise soleils* and other shading devices to protect the art.

Tiny inserts of stone in the shear walls link them symbolically to the garden, and a narrow slot of space behind the bed frames the treetops and gives the owner a retreat for a quiet nap on a Le Corbusier chaise. Palladino designed side tables and the steel base of the dining table, which were fabricated in LA by Gonzalo Algarate Design. Farrage contributed a burnished steel scroll over

the bedroom fireplace. Architect and client selected classic modern chairs and installed the varied artworks. The contractor, John Cordic of RJC Construction, was a graduate of the Southern California Institute of Architecture.

"The emphasis was on getting it right, not meeting deadlines," says Friesen. "If you have to finish in six months, you don't give the project its chance. At A&M we tried to sign the best artists and let them evolve, with just a little tweaking. I loved the process of talking back and forwards over a glass of wine. Michael let me play, but it's his house." The association is ongoing, for the architect is now working with Friesen on the remodeling of a classically inspired house in Montecito.

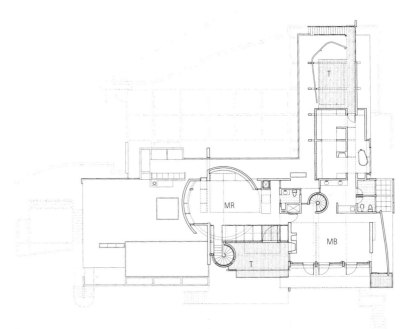

3 Second floor plan
4 Tightly coiled stair ascends to a gallery over the dining room
5 (overleaf) Spiral stair anchors the precisely articulated garden facade

3

4

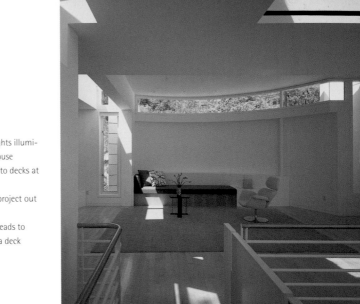

6 Clerestories and skylights illuminate every part of the house
7 The interiors open up to decks at both levels of the house
8 Cutaway shear walls project out into the entrance court
9 Second-floor gallery leads to master suite and out to a deck

2335

German precision and Japanese serenity mingle in a house that borders a canal. This idyllic enclave of landscaped waterways is a fragment of a failed real-estate venture of the 1910s—an attempt to recreate Venice beside the Pacific. A tall ficus hedge conceals the white stucco cube from the public footpath and the entrance off a service alley is impassive, but the interior is full of light and surprises. It's a machine for living that works in interesting ways and an experiment in minimalism that is enriched by views of water, sky, and greenery.

Holger Schubert, who grew up in Hamburg, trained as an industrial designer at Art Center and was planning to build on a beachfront plot when he chanced on the canals. He and his Japanese girlfriend, Yuriko Nagasaki, wanted to marry and raise a family and they decided that it would be quicker to remodel an existing house than to start from scratch. Schubert bought a ten-year-old, 2,800-square-foot contemporary residence, intending only to upgrade the kitchen and master bathroom. One thing led to another, and it took three years and half a million dollars to refine the entire house.

"I decided to tear out all the stuff we didn't like, saving whatever we could, and then design new window openings, built-ins, and finishes," he says. "I was naïve, thinking it was just a matter of drywall, glass, and paint." Imported windows and pivoting doors, limestone paving and white-oak paneling demanded expert installation. Schubert learned the hard way that few shared his sense of perfectionism, and that you don't demolish anything before deciding what to put in its place. "You have to know where you are going, or it's costly, time-consuming, and messy," he admits ruefully.

Now that the house is finished, harmony rules. In contrast to most neighboring residences, where the ground floor is for living and upstairs for sleeping, the couple's bedroom opens onto the enclosed garden, and the bathroom is suffused with natural light from a side wall of translucent glass that is screened by feathery bamboo. Both were inspired by Schubert's three-year sojourn in Tokyo working for the Toto corporation, where he learned to live with a minimum of possessions in one room, and cherish the alternation of light and shade, the sensuous and the austere.

1 An impassive entry facade, which opens onto the service alley
2 First, second and third floor plans

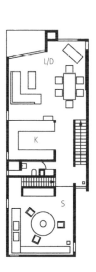
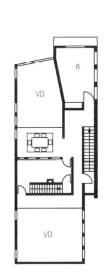

3

A deep soaking tub occupies much of the bathroom, and the open shower can be screened off by curtains. The floor slopes to a concealed strip drain and a mirror slides across on an overhead track. Essential tools, like electric toothbrushes and a water pic, are clamped to built-in storage cabinets above a pair of walnut-encased pedestal sinks. The bedroom ceiling was lowered to achieve intimacy and conceal a structural beam, and a flat television screen pivots on a central column so that it can be viewed from the bed or the facing sofa.

Aluminum-clad steps, lit from tiny downlights in the brackets that support the stainless steel handrail, lead up to the second-floor living areas and office, and to the upper-level guest bedroom, Japanese-style sitting room, and roof

terrace. The kitchen and dining area flow out of the double-height living room, and sunlight from eleven south-facing windows plays over the white walls and concrete floors. Expansive sliding windows to the west frame the canal. Schubert designed the dining table: a rectangle of medium density fiberboard with a matte white finish supported on two aluminum-wrapped poles set in the concrete. An opening at the center accommodates a metal container for *shabu shabu*, or a glass dish that can be illuminated from recessed spots directly above and below to cast shadows on the floor and ceiling. Sheer white organza drapes surround the twenty-foot-high office on three sides, turning it into what the designer calls "a floating work tent," and a circular pedestal table revolves

to keep the computer screen out of the sun. The table can get cluttered when two people are sharing it, but Schubert has acquired a space in Culver City for Archisis, his design practice.

As a first house by a designer with no architectural training, the project has turned out amazingly well. Schubert has given functionalism a human face, and he's constantly surprised by the way the house changes its character throughout the day. They wish they had more storage space, but realize they'd quickly fill whatever they had. Kaya, the couple's two-year-old daughter, has brought changes. "I love the sun, but for her it's too bright, so I've had to install drapes," admits Schubert. However, he is busily planning the beach house, incorporating the lessons he has learned from this one.

3 Expansive windows on the upper levels overlook the canal
4 Looking back from the living room to the open kitchen and gallery

5 Looking down on the office, wrapped in sheers like a cocoon
6 Felt seating pads and a ground-hugging table on the third floor
7 Walnut-clad sinks in the first floor Japanese-style bathroom
8 Pedestal dining table is pierced and lit from above and below

5

6

7

8

"I've always loved things that were silver and dynamic, but I wasn't smart enough to become a rocket engineer," says Edward Niles, who has been designing audacious houses out of his Malibu office for the past thirty-five years. "For me, architecture is sculpture and emotion—only if the client and I are excited can it happen." He likes to work on a grand scale, creating soaring, light-filled volumes and precisely engineered geometries of steel and glass. The 6,800-square-foot hilltop residence he built for Meyer and Doreen Luskin comprises three crystalline pavilions—for living, entertaining, and sleeping—linked by a curved gallery. Together, they embrace and mirror the landscape.

The clients bought the site for its spectacular views of the city, mountains, and ocean, intending to enhance the undistinguished house that came with it. When they learned that it would cost them almost as much to remodel as to rebuild, they resolved to commission something bold and interviewed several architects. Niles told them: "If I were you I wouldn't build on this site. Just put a tent on it and enjoy the natural beauty. But if you do decide to do something, I'll design it."

The challenge was to open the house up to the 360-degree views, giving every room a different orientation. The owners encouraged him to introduce curves and to use lots of glass, but insisted on a sense of security and protection from climatic extremes. Niles showed them study models and brought in his daughter, Lisa, and Steve Fernandez to work on the project. Each pavilion assumed a distinct shape and personality: a split cylinder that is divided between the lofty living room and low-ceilinged library; a truncated pyramid in which the dining room, kitchen, and a snug sitting area are juxtaposed; and the three linear volumes of the master suite, which are raised above an office and shelter a terrace. A succession of doors open onto a paved podium extending out to the lap pool, and the garage, guest rooms, and a greenhouse are tucked into the west side of the hill.

"Wherever you stand, you can understand the house as a whole," says Niles, whose ideas of breaking up the mass to achieve a more human scale were inspired by Wright. Here, he has achieved a remarkable sense of balance between the parts, which are firmly

1 The elliptical master bedroom commands a 360-degree view
2 Living room and library (left), kitchen, dining & family room (center), master suite over study (right)

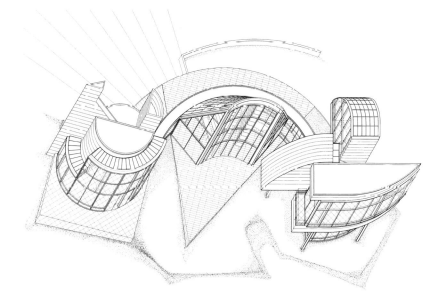

2

rooted yet fluid. As one walks around, looking through the transparent walls and noticing unexpected reflections, structure and landscape merge, dissolve, and are recomposed. In less expert hands, this experience could easily have been as disconcerting as stepping into a mirrored labyrinth, but the owners delight in the sense of tranquility and isolation it gives them. The tinted double glazing with its argon-filled core provides good insulation and protects them from glare, but can be opened at many points to admit a cooling breeze off the ocean, a few miles away. The thirty-foot-high expanse in the living room and in the central pavilion (which is partially screened by wood louvers) provides an exhilarating panorama of hills and sky. The west side is protected from the strong afternoon sun, and

three-quarters of its surface is clad with anodized aluminum panels.

Niles likens the exposed steel frame to a human skeleton that carries the weight and the musculature that holds everything in position. A massive column that rises through the living room like the center pole of a tent and is linked by slender ties to the perimeter structure should be able to withstand a force 8.0 earthquake and, simultaneously, a hundred-mile-an-hour gale. Elsewhere in the house, wide-flanged beams have been combined to form cruciform pillars, and the elegant steel mullions provide a feeling of strength in the glass walls. Other materials are used with similar consistency and integrity: limestone for the floors, sycamore for the cabinetry of the central pavilion, and straight-grain fir to bring warmth

to the inner walls of the master suite. A tapered wall of bookshelves with the profile of a sail turn the tall, narrow room adjoining the kitchen into an intimate retreat. The contractor was Marion Leard, and interior designer Audrey Alberts collaborated with Niles, subtly softening and enhancing the hard edges.

"Historically, Los Angeles has been one of the few places where individuals have been able to express themselves freely, though that freedom has been much eroded in the past twenty years by vigilante groups and building regulations," says Niles. "The Luskins, like all my clients, had the intellectual curiosity and the courage to stand out from the crowd."

3 Three linked pavilions embrace their reflections in the pool
4 Designer Audrey Alberts softened the steel-framed living room

4

5 Structure and landscape merge, dissolve, and are recomposed
6 Circulation areas mediate between the interior and exterior
7 Louvered shadows on the wall between dining room and kitchen

Frank Gehry once observed that most houses look their best while they are being framed, before the wood skeleton is covered with board and stucco, and, too often, disguised with ersatz period decor. A few architects make structure the star, exposing steel trusses, laminated beams, raw block and poured concrete, pushing the envelope as far as it will go.

Michael Jantzen is an artist-turned-inventor who has spent over thirty years developing systems that generate forms, most notably the prefabricated house he built as a weekend retreat for himself and his artist wife, Ellen. From the freeway climbing through the Tejon Pass on the route north to California's Central Valley, it can be glimpsed as a composition of folded planes clinging to a bare hillside—a site-specific art work, perhaps, like the yellow umbrellas that Christo scattered across these slopes a decade ago. Jantzen calls it a "hi-tech hut," a habitable sculpture that grew from models and a fascination with the idea of flexible, transformable architecture. "I like to think of houses as consciousness-raising devices," he says.

Like Buckminster Fuller, who designed the Dymaxion House, a light-weight aluminum cylinder suspended from a central mast, and the geodesic dome, Jantzen is exploring notions of prefabrication and portability. And, like Sam Rodia, the Italian-born plasterer who realized his vision of Watts Towers unaided, using only buckets and pulleys, Jantzen built the M-house entirely by himself. Working out of a garage in El Segundo, near Los Angeles International Airport, he fabricated seven eight-foot cubes of square steel tubing that were assembled on site as a structural frame. This is raised above the ground on steel pads that are anchored to concrete piles to withstand the hundred-mile-an-hour winds that can sweep the Techapi Mountains. Advanced Structures Incorporated provided the engineering expertise. Viroc boards (a patented mix of cement and wood fiber), spaced to admit light

and air, were attached to struts as sub-assemblies, trucked to the site, and attached to the frame. Every unit is folded in or out, like origami, the horizontal boards playing off the vertical, and seemingly arrested in motion. As Jantzen observes, "at the center of what appears to be an abstract, chaotic form, lies a simple, symmetrical structural base."

The outer carapace shades and protects an enclosure of insulated panels and tempered glass that is raised above ground on steel legs and reached by ramps. A pitched, skylit vault and glass doors that open up to shaded decks at either end make the interior feel much larger than its 400 square feet. It's a permeable space in fine weather and it provides an insulated retreat from summer heat and cold winds. Windows and

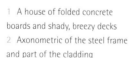
1 A house of folded concrete boards and shady, breezy decks
2 Axonometric of the steel frame and part of the cladding

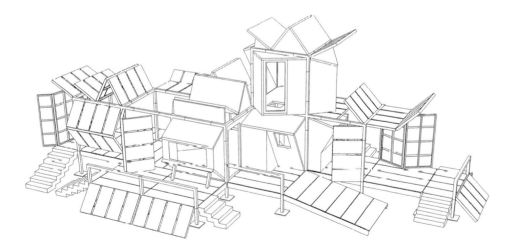

2

slots in the carapace frame pieces of the landscape and dapple the interiors with bars of sunlight, as though this were a solitary tree on the barren hillside. Panels are folded to provide an outdoor table and bench, and there's a built-in bed and desk. A sliding storage unit shuts the galley kitchen off from the sleeping area and doubles as a ladder leading up to the belvedere.

Inside and out, the cement boards are painted in a narrow spectrum of sage greens that pick up on the color of the hills after the winter rains and offer a refreshing contrast to the brown tones of fall. To achieve a seamless unity of structure, lining, and contents, the same colors are used for the cabinetry, fabrics, and even for Ellen Jantzen's paper bowls, which line a tapered shelf. The consistency induces a feeling of serenity; of being at one with nature.

The M-house is a kit of parts that could be disassembled and reconfigured on a different plot with a minimum of labor and site preparation. A wind generator, a pod with photovoltaic cells, a water storage tank, and propane gas tanks for cooking and back-up heating will be added to make the house energy self-sufficient. It requires little maintenance since the Viroc boards are resistant to fire and corrosion. Jantzen has already employed a similar system to build a garden pavilion, substituting stained mahogany for Viroc, but keeping the same spacing to achieve a pleasing play of shadow and light, shade and natural ventilation.

It is easy to imagine how this structure could be enlarged and how different materials and geometries could be plugged into it. Most systems of prefabrication use standardized parts in conventional assemblies that are too mundane and repetitive to win public acceptance, except as trailers. Jantzen has fused art and technology to offer unlimited possibilities for self-expression and customized forms. Even in its present modest form, the M-house would make an ideal beach cottage, sitting lightly on the land, withstanding storms and corrosive salt air.

3   A Constructivist artwork tightly anchored to a bare hillside
4   Built-in desk with a window commanding a panoramic view
5   Skylit bedroom in tones of sage that are used throughout
6   Kitchen storage cabinet/ladder leading up to the belvedere

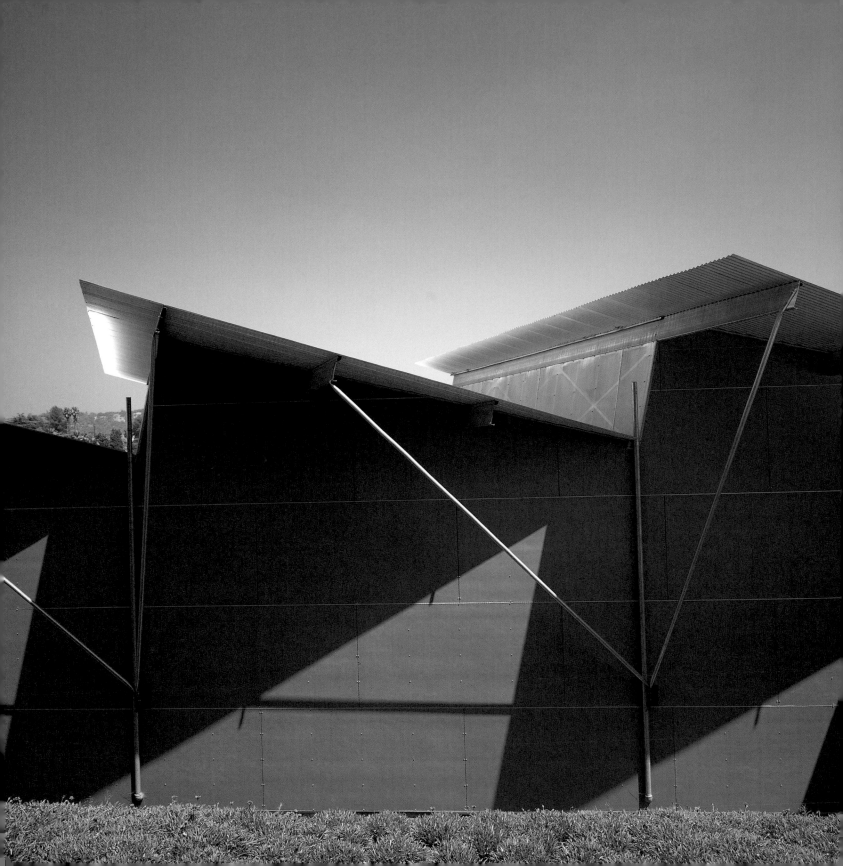

A century ago, art professors from the University of Southern California built weekend cottages in the hills midway between downtown LA and Pasadena, and that bohemian retreat evolved into Mount Washington, an unpretentious neighborhood of winding streets, eclectic houses, and a strong sense of community. Hubert Schmalix, an artist who came here from Austria in the late 1980s, bought a sloping site and commissioned a new house and studio from Alice Fung and Michael Blatt, a young architectural couple who live close by. He, his wife Fresnaida, and their two children wanted lofty, free-flowing living spaces opening up to the yard and views of the wilderness beyond. His priority was a spacious, well-lit painting studio. "It was basic stuff that gave us a lot of scope for design," says

Fung, who had worked with Blatt on much steeper slopes. They have just completed an emphatically vertical house for themselves.

Here the site was wide and stepped gently down. The architects decided to express the 2,300-square-foot house and 1,100-square-foot studio as separate buildings and cut away part of the hillside to accommodate the lower story below street level so that all the downstairs rooms would open onto the terrace and garden. That would keep the house well within the forty-five-foot height limit and satisfy the city plan that seeks to check overbuilding in Mount Washington. No caissons were required since it rests on bedrock, and the retaining wall was made a part of the house. The architects built the studio out from the slope as a steel-

framed volume clad in purple-sprayed Hardy board, with three bedrooms tucked in below. The end wall and three rectangles of corrugated steel that tip up over the skylights are rotated thirty degrees to face north, and the jagged protrusions cast angular shadows over the front wall. A galvanized V-channel supported on struts serves as a rain gutter that wraps around two sides of the studio.

To the right, a corrugated steel roof (ordered from a manufacturer of water tanks) arches over the entrance and loftlike living areas, which rotate in response to hillside. The curve plays off the angularity of the studio roofs and draws the eye downwards to the ground below. The wedge of space between the two upper floors serves as a carport and a view corridor—a reminder

1 Clerestories and projecting roofs on the north-oriented studio
2 Upper floor plan

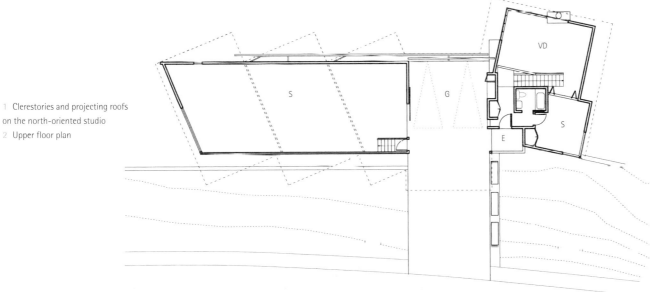

3

of when this cul-de-sac was a popular overlook point. Translucent Lexan is used for the entrance canopy and is screwed to the wood frame to serve as glazing, leaving only three conventional windows in the entire house. The goal was to select durable, inexpensive materials to achieve a raw aesthetic and make a clear distinction between the structure of steel and poured concrete and the skin of board, metal, and plastic that are screwed to the frame. "We played on repetitive forms we saw in Hubert's paintings," notes Fung, and Blatt saw it as a layering of materials, each with a separate character, and thought that "this would make a beautiful ruin."

The only material that strays from its natural state is the Hardy board. The architects had chosen purple, inspired by echium flowers that grow in the hills, as an accent in their own house, and Schmalix readily agreed to use it across his studio in preference to the dull gray of the unpainted board. For him, the interior of the house with its alternation of poured concrete and drywall, set off by handsome wood floors, is a bare canvas, to which he has added a vibrantly colored mural in the living room and a wall of purple linoleum in the master suite.

Multilevel interlocking living areas step down from the entrance and open onto a level terrace extending to the lap pool, which serves as a retaining wall for the landfill. The three bedrooms beneath the studio are rotated to express their independence of the steel frame, orient them to different points in the landscape, and break up the linear

walkway along the poured concrete retaining wall. Though it is intentionally rough-edged, the house was skillfully built by contractor Lewis Sullivan.

Schmalix is delighted with the lighting of his studio, which allows him to work long hours without distraction. However, as an émigré from northern Europe, he craves the sun and the sense of release that comes from stepping into a landscape of great beauty throughout the year.

3 Lower floor plan
4 Hubert Schmalix added a vibrant mural to the living room

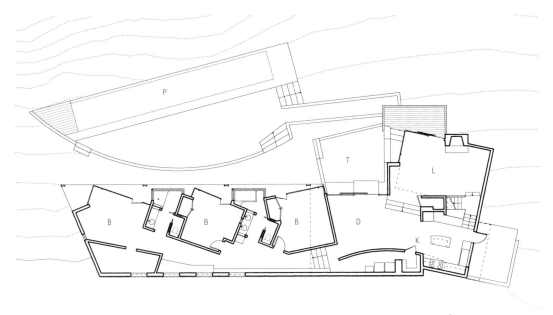

2

4

5 Bedrooms beneath the studio
open onto the pool terrace
6 The master bathroom is an open,
rough-edged sculpture
7 In contrast to the studio, the
house is clad in corrugated metal
8 Concrete walls and floor make
the master bedroom a cave

For Brian Murphy, the principal of BAM, "doing something new is the stimulus. We attract strong-minded clients and each job is driven by their needs and character." The most extreme example of this compulsion is the inward-looking steel house he built for Dennis Hopper in an edgy part of Venice, and repeatedly embellished. But Murphy sees a consistent sensibility in the firm's work, even as it swings from funky remodels to dashing new structures, from cool minimalism to a room with a blue floor and twenty red chandeliers. The beach-boy-turned-architect is part collagist, part inventor, part builder, transforming trash into treasures, and pushing everybody to be more adventurous.

Bert Berdis, a producer of radio commercials, and his wife Sherry Spees,

a tax lawyer, coveted the airy white house he built a decade ago for developer Patrick Prinster in the Hollywood Hills, but they were outbid. Instead, the couple bought a view site that was encumbered with a pretentious 1960s ranch house and invited Murphy and project architect Fro Vakili to remodel it. Their program was straightforward: a house for entertaining with an open kitchen they could both use, guest rooms for family, and an upstairs gallery where he could watch games on a big screen. The architects left the bedroom wing and the kidney pool, but took everything else down to the ground and rebuilt within the existing footprint to utilize the existing foundations, avoid the ordeal of seeking new permits, and save the expense of retaining walls and new footings.

Murphy never repeats himself, but he tried to infuse the spirit of Prinster— a cluster of lightweight metal pavilions— into the new 3,300-square-foot house. As he observes, "It is a blank into which all kinds of people can insert themselves and a beautiful foil for anything you want to put into it." Here, the architects pulled everything together under a single taut arc of steel that seems to hover weightlessly over the glass curtain wall. The beams and rafters are concealed beneath the inner plaster skin, but the vault gives the illusion of being as thin as an eggshell. Springy and light, the structure is reinforced to withstand seismic shocks and high wind on this exposed site. Steel ribs run horizontally rather than vertically, which increases the sense of transparency. As the architect notes,

1 The new structural frame arches over the existing pool
2 First floor plan

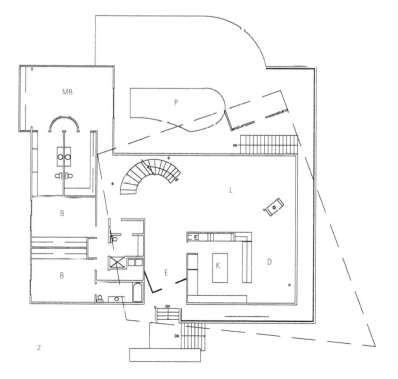

3 Freestanding hearth and flue in
the lofty living room
4 From below, the bowed roof
resembles a perfect wave

"The entire superstructure was rigged in the steel yard, then disassembled and reinstalled on site. Because of its quirky nature we had to be sure in advance that everything fitted together." Jim Davis of the Davis Development Group was the contractor.

For Murphy, an avid surfer, the bowed canopy is the perfect wave. It mirrors the dip of the canyon and is pulled down low at the southwest corner to block the sun until it drops behind the hills. At the southeast corner, the corrugated metal cladding is cut away over the pool, and three steel-mesh *brise soleils* wrap around the frame on the south and east sides, providing shade in summer but allowing the winter sun to warm the polished concrete floor and greatly reduce the need for radiant heating. (They also provide a footing for window washers). Though the house has air conditioning, it's rarely used, so effective is the cross ventilation. Energy efficiency allowed the architects to wrap glass around the living areas. Eight-foot-wide double-glazed sliders that correspond to the structural bays open the house to the pool.

Angled windows are set into the walls that flank the entry and the existing steps leading up from the motor court have been covered with diamond plate. A low foyer leads into the soaring, light-filled living room, within which the suspended mezzanine gallery and elegantly curved steel staircase seem airborne. As the clients requested, the hub of the living area is the open kitchen, which is spiced up by scarlet cabinetry. A stainless bar with a raised glass top and the dining table are mounted on casters so that they can be reconfigured for a catered buffet. A graceful metal chandelier is suspended from a swiveling steel arm attached to a column, and the freestanding hearth with its angled flue is silhouetted against the window wall—examples of how the architect is able to shift effortlessly from expansive gestures to small.

"I wish there more people who wanted to dance to this kind of music, rather than worry about resale or what their mother-in-law would think," remarks Murphy.

5 The low-ceilinged foyer leads into the living room

6 An elegant stair ascends to the suspended mezzanine

7 Murphy designed the stainless sink in the powder room

Finn Kappe grew up in the landmark house Ray Kappe designed for his family in the mid-1960s: a habitable bridge of laminated redwood beams lofted on concrete towers above the slope of Rustic Canyon in west Los Angeles. "I learned as much as I could from my father," he says, "the honest expression of simple materials in a home that relates to and incorporates its surroundings. I never wanted to copy him but, rather, to find a way of my own." The son realized that goal most decisively in the house he built for his wife (Maureen Tamuri, from whom he has separated) and daughter high up in Topanga Canyon—a wilderness setting that is remote in spirit from the metropolis that surrounds it.

The house was designed to be tough and defensive on the outside, resistant to high winds, brush fires, and mud slides; also shutting out the highway and a neighboring house. "I wanted to build something that was tough and gritty, not smooth and pretty," says Kappe. "I could have cut and filled, but I preferred to move as little earth as possible and perch it above the ground." The 3,800-square-foot, L-plan house backs up to a twenty-foot-high retaining wall of concrete block at the top of the slope, and is raised above most of the area it covers. A boldly expressed steel frame, supported on caissons where the land drops away, engages four block walls, which reach out to frame views of the ravine to the west.

The steel columns taper downwards to dramatize the shift from lateral thrust to perpendicular load, and projecting beam ends are tapered to suggest movement. The concrete block walls are raked to evoke rock strata and to express the pull of gravity. A corrugated sheet of galvanized metal on one side may some day be turned into a water feature. The main house rotates away from the side wing, with its studio and two second-floor bedrooms, so that the two appear to be splitting apart. Raw and muscular though the structure is, it sits comfortably in the rugged landscape and never feels overpowering, even when you are standing close up to it. Kappe thinks it would make an impressive ruin, if a fire were to melt the steel and glass, leaving only the walls standing.

Steps lead up to the entrance and down to a sunken sitting area that soars thirty-six feet high. The wall of glass opening onto a redwood deck,

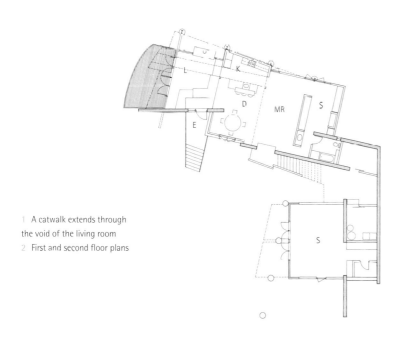

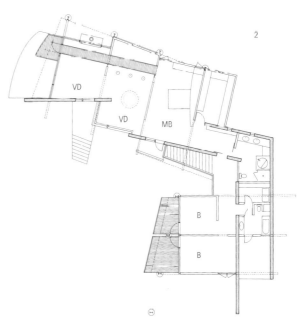

1 A catwalk extends through the void of the living room
2 First and second floor plans

3

the red-painted I-beams, polished concrete floor, and striated block walls protect you from the elements while releasing you into the landscape. As darkness falls, the open hearth feels like a campfire, drawing you into its warm embrace. Glass wraps around the corner dining area, across from the open kitchen. This is tucked beneath a steel-and-redwood catwalk extending out through the glass to a little balcony and running back to the mezzanine gallery that links the master bedroom to those in the side wing. A family room and study are located beneath this gallery, and all the plumbing and mechanical equipment is concentrated in a ten-foot-wide bar extending along the rear side of the house on both levels.

For Kappe, as with many architects who build a house for themselves, this was a laboratory in which to test ideas and materials before trying them out on clients. He played riffs on the design as he does on his guitar, allowing it to grow in response to the land. This organic process may be hard to achieve elsewhere, for Topanga is an anomaly in Southern California—a haven for libertarians, with no design controls. Though he had only a third of the financial resources he needed at the start, he was able to realize his vision by doing much of the work himself, spreading it out over two years, and using recycled materials—like the big ceiling fan that evacuates hot air. Cross ventilation keeps the house cool through the hot months, though the interior can become uncomfortable when the windows are left closed on a hot day—an inevitable trade off for leaving the windows unshaded. In winter, the concrete floors absorb sunlight, and there is little need for the radiant heating. However, Kappe is planning to supplement the passive solar heating with solar panels connected to a storage tank.

The lessons learned here are being applied to a powerful but refined house that Kappe is currently completing in a canyon above Beverly Hills.

3 Structural steel and walls of glass in the living room
4 Main house and bedrooms over a studio in the side wing

5 Looking out to the canyon from
the corner dining area
6 Open kitchen and counter tucked
in beneath the catwalk

When Michael Rotondi broke away from Morphosis in 1991, he and Clark Stevens set up a new office in The Brewery, a twenty-three-acre industrial estate on the northeast edge of downtown LA. Contractor Richard Carlson had bought the abandoned plant, turned it into a live-work complex for artists, and moved into an electrical cable shop that was sandwiched between the brewery and a rail yard. He lived there for eight years with his wife, Kathy Reges, who breeds show dogs and collects contemporary art. She saw the edgy, but comfortable Tieger house, which RoTo had designed for an art collector in Morristown, N.J., and gave her husband an ultimatum: hire the architects to remake this thirty-four-foot high loft space, or find a house on the Westside.

Memory and improvisation are the twin themes of the steel structure that grew out of the masonry box. It celebrates the industrial legacy of the site and serves as a landmark to anchor the generic warehouses to the north, while shutting out the fumes and noise of diesel trains with a massive steel baffle. Construction documents were kept to a minimum, and much of the detailing was left to workers who were challenged to be inventive and make best use of salvaged steel. An oil storage tank was sawn in half to serve as a lap pool; another contains a shower and rises through the roof to become a belvedere. Massive I-beams were craned in and welded to the structural frame, which was rooted in the ground beyond the existing concrete walls to ensure stability. Fifty years before, Charles and

Ray Eames ordered the parts for their Case Study house from catalogues, assembling the frame, infill panels, and windows as precisely as a jigsaw puzzle. Here, the process was more akin to sculpture, even though the underlying concepts were rigorously architectural.

Rotondi and Stevens listened intently to their clients' desires—for a comfortable living environment that would be visually electrifying, with a spacious gallery at ground level and private living quarters above. Once the program was set, the architects studied the existing building and its relationship to the site. "We deciphered its genetic code, and realized we could create new openings and achieve an organic relationship between parent and progeny," Rotondi explains. They sketched furiously, developing a proportioning

1 The existing loft space is now utilized as an art gallery
2 Plan of the upper living area

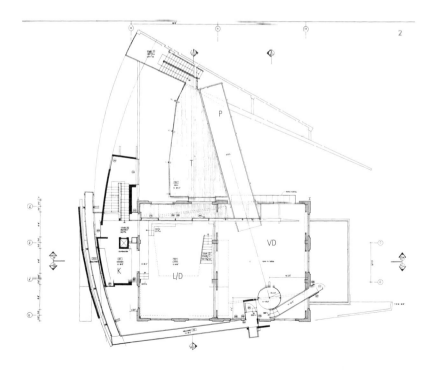

system that the body would respond to, and overlaying the existing orthogonal geometry with a radial baffle and roof plane. They drew lines that connected the house to the natural and built landscape, drawing on the experience of designing a new university in South Dakota for the Lakota Native American tribe, which believes that everything is interconnected by lines of force.

The 6,000-square-foot house works on multiple levels: as a stack of interconnected spaces woven together by stairs and walkways that are threaded through a bamboo grove, behind the baffle (which doubles as a sun shade), and extend out on a pool deck that is raised on pipe columns, sixteen feet above the ground. The pool is aligned on Library Tower, the tallest building in LA, and points back to a window slot that frames Mount Baldy, on the northeast horizon. The steel is softened by foliage, and plays off the classic proportions of the century-old cable shop. The gallery retains a raw industrial character, with the original rail tracks and ceiling trusses, and new pivoting doors opening onto a walled courtyard so that hundreds of guests can move freely indoors and out. Jutting into this volume is the glass-enclosed tip of the lap pool, and the vertical tank, which is cut away to serve as a chimney that evacuates hot air.

In contrast to this uncompromisingly tough space, the lofty living room is warmed by a cherry-wood floor and by the earthy tones of the walls. As the architects collaborated with Carlson on the construction, April Greiman, a celebrated graphic designer who is married to Rotondi, worked with Reges on the colors. She sought to create connective tissue between wood and steel, selecting anubis (a dark purple-brown) and related hues for the sculptured fireplace and the mezzanine-level guest room, which reads as a box suspended within the larger volume. Reges was initially shocked, but sought a second opinion from artist friends and was won over. The master bedroom has the cozy feel of an attic, tucked in beneath the corrugated roof planes and a projecting I-beam, with a four-poster bed on casters that can be positioned to take advantage of the light in every season.

3 A steel baffle protects the house from noise and fumes
4 Staircase leads from the living room to a guest bedroom

5 Cherry wood floors play off a corrugated metal ceiling
6 Section: heavy lines indicate additions to the old plant
7 Catwalk between the masonry structure and steel baffle

5

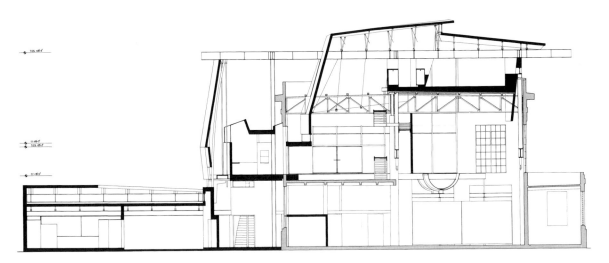

6

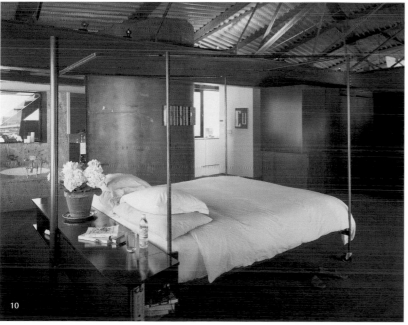

8 Cutaway oil drum evacuates hot
air from the art gallery
9 A second steel drum was halved
to create a lap pool
10 A four-poster on casters in the
atticlike master bedroom

FRONTING THE OCEAN

Winter storms, mud slides, occasional brush fires, a torrent of traffic along the coast highway, neighbors pressing in from either side: there's a price to be paid for living where the mountains meet the Pacific. The beachfront communities south of Santa Monica are tamer, but crowded. The wonder of the ocean outweighs all the drawbacks and architects respond to the challenge.

Perched on hills that roll (and sometimes crumble) down to the coast above Sunset Boulevard, Castellammare is as romantic as its name—no wonder J. Paul Getty built his villa and museum there. Jerry and Doreen Rochman, psychoanalysts with a sharp eye for beauty, were shaken out of their house by the Northridge earthquake and moved to another that was poorly designed but commanded dizzying views up and down the coast. Their children had moved away, and they were looking for "an architectural wonder" with an open plan and lots of places to step outside.

Patiently, they considered the possibilities, explored three houses by Franklin Israel, and commissioned him to do a radical remodel. He began sketching a concept just before his death in 1996, leaving Barbara Callas and Steven

Shortridge, the partners who have built on his legacy, to develop the design and bring it to completion. Annie Chu, a former Israel associate, also had a hand in the design, but most of the credit goes to Callas and project architect David Spinelli. They saved the garage but leveled the rest, extending the new construction to the edge of the slope and tucking the master suite and a second deck below the living areas.

In a neighborhood of Mediterranean mansions standing tall, the 3,000-square-foot Rochman house is an anomaly, and it's almost invisible. The reticent single-story facade of steel-troweled stucco is largely concealed behind a tall hedge and is designed to shut out traffic noise. A parapet conceals the flat roof, a tilted canopy frames the cavelike entrance,

and there's a single window-skylight. The garage and entry doors are faced with zinc, which fades into the gray-green walls, and both pick up on the tones of the vegetation and the Santa Monica Mountains. Nothing prepares you for the spectacle within.

A wall of polished brown stucco tilts over the stairs, and a row of cabinets leads to a tiny consulting room with the obligatory two doors, where Mr. Rochman can meet with patients when he is not at the office. Step forward and you feel you are in a wide-screen movie, enjoying a 180-degree panorama of ocean and mountains. Windows on two sides of the living room are tilted inwards to draw your eyes down while holding you back from the edge, to evoke the prow of a ship heading out to sea, and, more

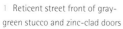
1 Reticent street front of gray-green stucco and zinc-clad doors
2 Ground floor plan

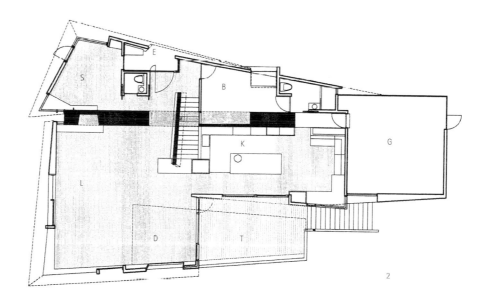

practically, reduce the need for cleaning. A window bench is tucked into the mitered glass corner. Sliders open the kitchen up to the deck, which is shaded by a cedar trellis that flows in through the glass to provide a visual link between the indoor and outdoor dining areas. What's remarkable is how the house exploits its site and views but is also inward-looking and protective, with a formal sitting area centered on the hearth. The master bedroom leads out onto an expansive cedar deck that is cantilevered out from the skewed corner of the house and extends back to a Jacuzzi built into the hillside. A tree grows through the slats and the balustrade is clear glass, giving you the feeling you are airborne.

"You can't compete with this view, so we tried to control the framing of it," says Callas, "lifting the windows off the floor so that you feel that the water is coming under you. Cross ventilation provides cool air year-round, but we had to control the flow—it can get very windy. The geometry of house was dictated by setbacks and the configuration of site, as well as a very strong influence from Rudolph Schindler."

The house was worth the seven-year wait. Every part of it is precisely shaped, as though it had been carved from a solid block, with a harmonious balance of solid and void, and axes that tie the varied spaces together. The maple floors, vertical-grain Douglas fir cabinetry, and warm white walls soften the sharp angles and become an integral part of the whole. It was impeccably constructed by Ralph Herman of Herman Construction, and every detail is meticulously crafted.

Jerry Rochman, who got his first taste of modernism when he bought an Eames chair in his native Chicago at age fifteen, was a passionate client, who was closely involved in the process. "We met every Saturday over several months in design discussions with Frank," he recalls. "We felt he wasn't going far enough but finally he understood we wanted a special house—no halfway measures. To do something like this you should form a relationship with your architects that will last forever."

3 Window bench provides a high-level view of cliffs and ocean
4 Steps lead down from the living areas to the garden and a deck

4

5 At the corner of the house, a
cedar deck leads up to a Jacuzzi
6 The master bedroom opens up to
the ocean through sliders
7 In the living room, a sitting area
is centered on the hearth
8 The open kitchen serves indoor
and outdoor dining areas

Peg Yorkin co-founded the Feminist Majority Foundation, which lobbies for women's rights and recently took over *Ms.* magazine. She had a beach house in Malibu beach, but decided to buy the double lot next door on which to build a more expansive weekend retreat she could share with Nicole and David, her adult children, and their families. "It was a joint project," she recalls. "Not the easiest thing to do, except that I controlled the purse strings. We considered several architects before meeting Buzz Yudell, looking at two of his courtyard houses, and agreeing on him."

They asked for a diversity of public spaces, flowing together and out to the deck, providing for intimate and large-scale gatherings, and three master suites on the second floor, giving each member of the family a private space looking out to the ocean. (This was a great gain for David Yorkin, who had to make do with a room on the highway in the old house). There was to be a screening room, lots of storage space, and quiet places to read or write. The house had to satisfy the son's preference for modern and the daughter's for a more traditional look, with mother occupying neutral ground. Above all, it had to be unpretentious and serene. Yudell headed a team comprising partner John Ruble, project architect Marc Schoeplein (who has since set up his own practice and converted a Beverly Hills loft into the Feminist Majority's offices), and Tina Beebe, who helped select colors, materials, and plantings.

Serenity starts on the sidewalk, with rows of beach pebbles set like speed bumps into the pavers that lead to a gate in the wall enclosing a courtyard landscaped with beach grasses, a fountain for white noise, and a boardwalk. Right away, the sound of traffic is muted, and you begin to decompress; that feeling is strengthened as you step inside the house and pick up a murmur of the surf. The brilliant light draws you forward past the staircase that leads up to the second floor and a cross axis that extends through the living area to the kitchen. Integrally colored, steel-troweled stucco in soft tones warms the space and shimmers softly. The house unfolds as a series of layers, expanding in scale until it finds release in the expansive deck (half covered, half open) and the immensity of the ocean. The water is reflected in the sliders so that, from certain viewpoints, it appears to be flowing around the house.

1 The highway facade is boldly modeled with projecting bays
2 First floor plan

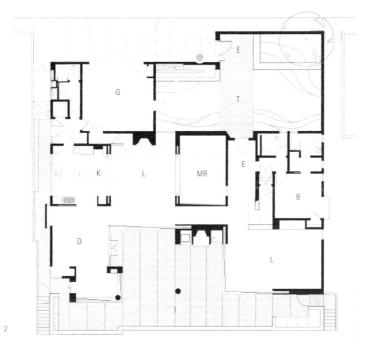

2

For Yudell, who loves to abstract the vernacular or make subtle references to historic architecture, this may be his most convincingly modern building. The highway facade is boldly modeled, with projecting bays and rooftop light scoops, while flat roof and horizontal steel glazing bars on the ocean side evoke the marine modernism of 1920s, though without the pipe railings and rounded corners. The architect praises the sophistication of the client and the way they found common ground. Most people crave ornament and historical references, either because they feel uncomfortable with pure form and surface, or because they want to project an image of status and confuse show with substance. And yet, for all its restraint, this is a house of extraordinary richness and subtlety.

The architects have expressed their customary preference for discrete spaces that interconnect but are clearly defined and can be closed off. Nowhere is this more evident than in the master suites, each of which is like a little house within the house, staggered to give each an unbroken panorama of ocean. The first two are separated by the main staircase, which is lined with translucent glass and sliding panels of blue and purple glass that borrow light from either side to project a magical glow, while giving privacy to the dressing areas they screen. Two children's bedrooms separate this pair from Ms. Yorkin's suite, with its arched portal and curved soffits that simulate waves—in tones of aqua, eau de nil, and blue-white.

Fort Hill Construction built the 7,500-square-foot house superbly well,

and interior designer Jan Snyder helped select the furnishings. However, because the architects were closely involved at every stage, playful and practical touches abound. Curved amber sconces emerge from the walls, and translucent squares are suspended over downlights between exposed joists. Ribbed glass on the fronts of the kitchen cabinets admit light through from the translucent backs. Bronze baseboards protect the stucco. But, for all the beauty, you feel that this is a house to live in—most obviously in the screening room, which has the character of a snuggery—and in the sun-bathed breakfast room, which was abandoned in favor of the kitchen counter, and is now Ms. Yorkin's favorite retreat.

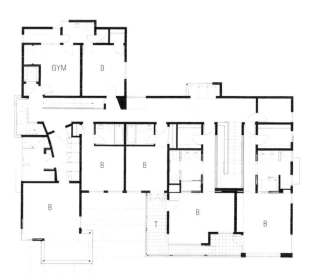

4

3 Three bedroom suites in staggered formation face the ocean
4 Second floor plan
5 (overleaf) The living room flows out through sliders onto the deck

6

6 Sliding, backlit panels of colored
glass flank the main staircase
7 Wavelike soffits in watery tones
animate the owner's bedroom
8 The spacious kitchen can be
closed off with pocketing doors
9 Curved, amber wall sconces
softly light the bedroom corridor

In his fifty years of practice, Ray Kappe has built over a hundred houses, and designed many more, most within an easy drive of his own landmark house in Pacific Palisades. He's a master of interlocking spaces and carefully modulated light, and strove for energy efficiency long before that became a widespread concern. The 2,600-square-foot beach house he designed for Samuel Culbert, a professor of management at UCLA, and his wife, Rosella Forte, has a simplicity that distills a lifetime of shaping living spaces to people and sites.

There's a stoplight on the coast highway that allows you to pause and glimpse the rounded roof of the house and its impassive facade of gray-green stucco rising from a steel frame above the double garage, with a narrow slot of glass to one side. It's crisp and enigmatic, a petrified wave that could have sprung from the surf. The same integrally colored, steel-troweled plaster is carried inside, together with the exposed, silver-painted steel frame, so that the substance and structure of the house are made tangible. The master bedroom and adjoining office open up through sliders to the ocean that pounds at the pilings, twenty feet below. A cantilevered staircase leads up to the second floor living areas and a deck that juts out over the water. Spare rooms on the highway side are tucked in beneath a third-level mezzanine gallery from where you can glimpse the horizon and the promontory of Palos Verdes through a long dormer window set into the curved roof.

The curves were one of the requests that Culbert made when he selected Kappe to remodel the duplex that formerly occupied this site. He had plenty of experience in reconfiguring and extending other houses he and his family had lived in and knew exactly what he wanted here.

The priorities were to see the ocean from everywhere in the house and not to hear the highway traffic, as well as a sense of openness and smooth, rounded surfaces. It was a simple program that he could have executed himself with a builder and someone to sign off on the plans, but Kappe worked closely with him to infuse it with poetry and practicality.

Though little of the existing structure was left untouched, the house qualified as a remodel and occupies the same footprint as before. There is a strict height limit on beach houses, and a flat roof would not have provided

1 Impassive, steel-troweled stucco façade on the coast highway
2 First and second floor plans

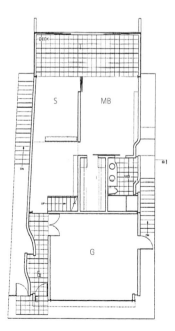

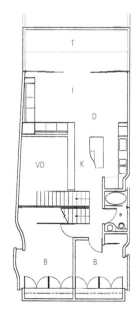

2

enough headroom for the mezzanine gallery. However, you can go four feet higher if you have a monopitch or gable roof. Kappe sketched the wave, which pleased the client and brought the same height bonus. Culbert suggested an earth tone for the plaster, but the architect persuaded him that it would be more appropriate if they were to take their cues from the ocean, rather than the land. The owners wanted a modern house that felt warm, and this was achieved with the oak floors and stair treads, the folding shutters that can be used to darken the master bedroom or the office, and the built-in cabinets and wall sofa in the living area.

To eliminate the barrier between house and ocean, the aluminum-framed sliders on both levels can be stacked to open the entire south front

to the elements. At the lower level, quarter-inch steel rods support taut cables to create an unobtrusive barrier; at the upper, there's a railing of clear glass at the edge of the deck and sand-blasted side panels to provide privacy and a windbreak. The stairs and mezzanine are also railed in clear glass, and, since the second floor is cut away around the staircase, you can look down and get a sense of the entire house from the upper level. As a result, the interior can feel as outdoorslike and breezy as a ship's deck, and the sense of infinite expansion is heightened by the experience of entering through a narrow paved foyer, lit from a narrow slot of glass beside the door and compressed by a gently curved wall. A window at the top of the stairs frames a hill that echoes the arch of the wave.

"There were many agreeable surprises," says Culbert. "The house is refreshing for its simplicity. We chose concrete over granite for the countertops, and there are no fancy finishes. However, the plaster is so beautiful that we are reluctant to hang art on the walls. Best of all, it's the most energy-efficient house you could imagine; there is almost no need for heating or cooling."

3 Wavelike section of the house
4 Looking back through the office to the narrow entry foyer
5 (overleaf) The living room opens onto a jutting, glass-enclosed deck

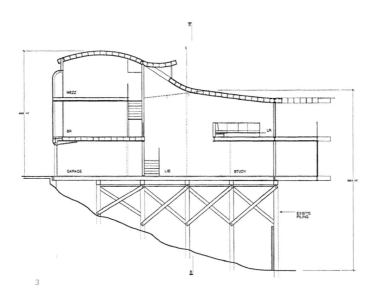

3

5

6 The master bedroom can be darkened with folding shutters
7 Staircase to the mezzanine gallery beneath the wave vault
8 Looking down to the living area and out through dormer

Dean Nota worked for Ray Kappe before setting up his own practice and learned a lot from that veteran architect about the manipulation of space and light, though his own houses are more minimal and abstract. Tony Reyna, a health-care consultant, picked him to design a beachfront house, partly because he lived close by, and partly because he admired Nota's Naiditch house, which occupies another kind of edge site in Altadena, looking out to the San Bernardino Mountains. Reyna wanted the same combination of privacy and openness for his house, which is separated from the sand by a popular walkway. The Culbert house opens up to the waves, Reyna's to waves of people. The client wanted places to entertain friends and feel at one with the ocean, but also a quiet, airy retreat.

The concept came quickly: a three-level, 3,450-square-foot house, with a wall of glass facing west to frame the ocean and a stucco facade that backs onto a street. It replaced a ruinous brick block that may have been the first building to go up on this stretch of the shore. The glass is tilted inwards to make room for a walled forecourt that provides a small degree of separation from the public, and the jutting balconies are a nod to the lifeguard shelters on the shore. The rear is tilted out beyond the building line to provide extra space above the garage, and the roof is curved down at front and back, like a tipped hat brim. This wedge configuration gives the house a graceful profile and a light, springy quality as compared to the dumb developers' boxes that have grabbed every permissible inch on the neighboring sites. "I carved away at the mass of the house, sacrificing a little space to articulate the exterior," says Nota. The glass, which shimmers in the sun and glows like a giant lantern at night, de-materializes the house, which is further lightened by a shift in the color of the stucco, from gray-green on the outside to a sandy gray within.

The entry passage along the north side leads into a media room that opens into the walled forecourt and an open, dark red steel stair with slate treads lit from a wall of glass block. You emerge into an explosion of space and light: the two-story living room that seems to project out through the wall of glass to engage the beach and the sky. The hearth provides an anchor, the deck serves as a front stoop from which to

1 Balconies are cantilevered out from a tilted glass facade
2 Second and third floor plans

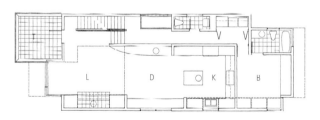

chat with neighbors and observe the passing throng. The dining-kitchen area is located under the third-floor master suite, which extends back past a dressing area to a bathing room with a Jacuzzi and a skylit steam shower. A bridge leads down one side of the void to a deck that is bisected by glass, half inside, half out. For Nota, the curved ceiling is an organizing device, controlling the elements beneath. It evokes a gentle swell, rather than a wave.

From the beach, you suppose that the house must have the character of a goldfish bowl; within it feels tranquil and protected, except when you step up to glass or onto the lower deck. You quickly realize that passersby have other things to look at and that the floors cut into their angle of view. The master suite seems as private as if it

were located on a walled estate, but mirrors to either side pull in views. Motorized blinds can be lowered to black out the interior or block the westerly sun, so that Reyna can easily determine the mood and the lighting level. The warm white of the interior and the maple floors are accented with colors, like the two tones of limestone in the master suite, and the reddish cherry kitchen and dining room cabinets that dramatize the spatial shifts. Interior designer Marina Mizruh helped with the colors; Nota and Reyna chose the classic modern furnishings. Baldwin Construction did an exemplary job on the finishes, which convey a sense of luxury that's rare in a beach house.

"Working at the beach, I've learned to be prudent with materials," says Nota. "It's just like a boat—you don't

want the crew to be out there painting every six months. Stucco, concrete, painted aluminum, and hot-dipped galvanized steel are OK. But wood and even stainless steel can pose problems, and paints get weaker and weaker, now that toxic ingredients have been banned. Here, we've tried to use durable materials that will age gracefully."

3 Side and rear of the house from the walkway to the beach
4 Looking from the living room to the ocean at twilight

5 Dining room and kitchen, tucked
beneath the master suite
6 Master bedroom, looking back to
dressing area and bathroom

6

1

"In a minimalist house there's much more than meets the eye," says Andy Neumann. "The details—in the drawings and construction—have to be perfect. We don't get the chance to do this very often in Santa Barbara County—most people want a Spanish colonial or a Tuscan villa because it's easier to sell."

The architect, who surfs from his own beachfront and has designed fifty houses at the shore in his thirty years of practice, responded enthusiastically to what started out as a modest commission: extending a 900-square-foot guest house to serve as a weekend retreat for a couple who divide their time between LA and New York. Susan Sullivan is an actress, who played the mother-in-law on *Dharma and Greg*, besides starring in movies and off-Broadway. Connell Cowan, her companion, is a psychologist who writes and sculpts, and the two were intent on creating an object of beauty on an ideal, traffic-free site that flows onto the beach and is backed by a marsh that is protected as a wildlife sanctuary.

The original house was designed by Jack Warner for the son of the lady who lived on the neighboring lot, so the accommodations were minimal and there was no kitchen—a must for Cowan, who loves to cook. It was set far back from the beach with narrow windows at front and back to frame a glimpse of hills and ocean. The new owners wanted to open up the house and achieve the feeling of an artist's loft and a purity of line that would serve as a foil to their collection of contemporary art and Asian furniture. They turned to Neumann because, as Sullivan recalls, "he had an affinity to the ocean and we didn't feel intimidated by him." It took time to secure the required permits and so the job stretched out as a leisurely collaboration between Neumann and his project architects, Dave Mendro and Bob Pester, both clients, and the contractor, Frank Louda (who has now turned over his firm to Tom Jackson).

They decided not to push forward as far as they could but to add an upstairs master suite that would have a view over the seawall of granite boulders. This was placed over the new living room at the front, since the original house, which now contains a dining area and guest bedroom, had to be raised three feet to reduce the risk of flooding and the second story had to remain under the twenty-foot height

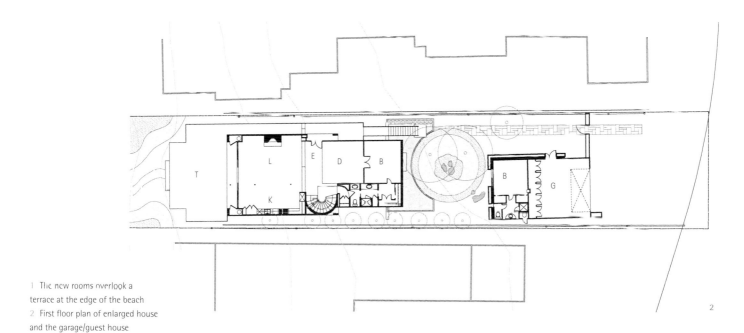

1 The new rooms overlook a terrace at the edge of the beach
2 First floor plan of enlarged house and the garage/guest house

2

3

limit. In raising the wood-frame structure on hydraulic jacks, it was also shifted slightly to align with the detached garage/guest bedroom in back. The old house telescopes into the new, which is five feet wider; all three structures are tied together with a new skin of Synergy, a soft gray acrylic-finished plaster, chosen for its resistance to cracking. The space between the two guest rooms is landscaped with a circular moss garden that frames three standing basalt crystals, in homage to Isamu Noguchi. The supporting wall of the old cottage is masked by a CorTen base and a moat.

Two steps mark the divide between the old, with its exposed joists and original window, and the new, which opens up to the ocean through a wall of glass, providing a spacious 2,680-square-foot

interior. A radiant-heated concrete floor and white walls tie the two volumes together, and glass sliders pocket to open the living room to a terrace and grasses on the sand, and the master bedroom to a balcony. Circular openings are punched out of the projecting roof plane, as skylights in the old house, and over a tightly coiled spiral stair with fanned glass treads, which seem to disappear. A planned counter was eliminated so that the kitchen is one wall of the living room, and visitors who might have perched on high stools when they are inside, now flop into sybaritic white armchairs. The most theatrical gesture is the tub in her bathroom, placed up against a wall of clear glass—though blinds can be lowered when the beach is exposed at low tide.

"Andy was full of ideas, but this was a true collaboration—he was delighted with our input," says Sullivan. Neumann concurs. "For the clients, and especially Connell who has an artist's eye, this was an art project," he says. "They wanted to change and refine everything, and, though the budget was tight at the start, they took their time and never cut corners."

3 The kitchen is an integral part of the spacious living room
4 The dining room, lit from an oculus, is within the old shell

5 Bathing *au naturel*; blinds roll
down for privacy at low tide
6 Sybaritic seating complements
the linear Asian furniture
7 Top-lit spiral stair with glass
treads leads to the master suite

ENGAGING THE LANDSCAPE

Every good house tries to relate to its surroundings, which are sometimes entirely natural: mature trees, the walls of a canyon, or hilltop views. These five houses are shaped by the landscape—expansive or contained, austere or gentle. A steel-framed house protected by rooftop pools contrasts with a woodsy remodel that plays off the trees surrounding it.

Barton Myers, the veteran urbanist and architect of grand public buildings, is a dedicated modernist, but when he and his wife, Vicki, moved to LA they became very attached to their Spanish hacienda high above the Hollywood Bowl. What drew them away was the chance to build a new 6,000-square-foot complex on a forty-acre slope at the head of a secluded canyon in Montecito, eighty miles northwest. Now, their nearest neighbors are rattlesnakes and coyotes, and in place of July 4th fireworks there is the spectacle, many nights of the year, of stars in a black void and illuminated oil rigs glittering like fireflies in the Santa Barbara Channel.

The new house is as different from the old as its setting, but it returns to a theme Myers explored thirty years ago, soon after opening his first office in Toronto. There he built his family a contemporary steel-and-glass house on a site hemmed in by redbrick Victorians and later designed the Wolf house—an elegant, transparent loft in a parklike setting, raised above the ground on steel columns. Fond memories of those early efforts spurred a desire to attempt something more ambitious, yet equally pared down.

"I began thinking about early Wright houses, Rudolph Schindler's studio house in West Hollywood, and the Barcelona Pavilion of Mies van der Rohe—simple arrangements of walls enclosing living spaces and gardens," Myers recalls. "Charles and Ray Eames used steel and glass components out of builders' catalogues for their landmark house in Pacific Palisades and that was a major inspiration. I thought—as so many modern architects have—that this singular house might serve as a prototype for high-density affordable housing."

To conserve the beauty of the landscape and save its trees, Myers (who shared the role of contractor with his wife) decided to put his studio at the top of the steep slope, a guest house and garage below, and the main house on a level pad between. Lofty steel-framed pavilions have roll-up segmented glass doors opening onto terraces and roll-down steel shutters to provide security when the owners are away, to protect from brush fires, and screen the sun. As an added safeguard and to insulate the interiors from the heat of summer, each flat roof serves as a shallow pool, containing water that is recirculated from uphill storage tanks. Nature conditions the air, and a lap

1 Shallow roof pools protect from brush fires and insulate interiors
2 Site plan of studio (a), main house (b), guest house (c), and garage (d)

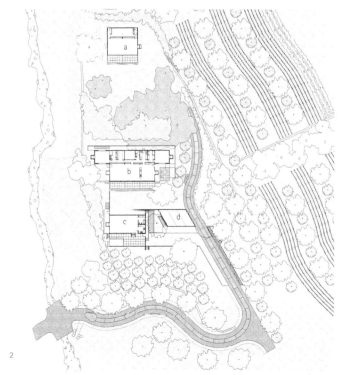

2

pool runs along the edge of the guest-house roof.

Simplicity pays off in these stripped-down loft spaces. The great luxury is height, which brings uphill views and well balanced light through clerestory windows in the studio and the living-dining area of the house. A cantilevered canopy over the south front shuts out the midday sun in summer, but allows it to warm the interior in winter. There is no need for drapes or blinds, for the sides of the canyon form a natural enclosure, and the nearest house is far below. Master and guest bedrooms occupy low wings beside and behind the living area, and are separated by bath and service rooms. These are linked by a corridor that runs behind double-sided book stacks. Unpretentious furnishings and area rugs are scattered across polished concrete floors.

As in the Eames House, hard surfaces and sharp angles are softened by the play of light and reflections of greenery. A water spout from the roof of the guest house creates a soothing murmur. Trees and boulders flank the three pavilions, tying them to the earth. The house was built inexpensively, and its boldly exposed, galvanized structure should require little maintenance. It's as functional as a factory, but its grand proportions evoke classical temples and Palladian villas, and it puts a fresh spin on the California tradition of airy porticoes jutting forward from adobe masses. Here, the entire living space stands in for the portico, with its welcome shade and constant breezes, and the bedrooms and service core with their solid rear walls have something of the adobe. Locals are obsessed with

building in Spanish Colonial style; Myers has eliminated the ornamental overlay and has burrowed to the roots of that tradition, creating shelter and shade on a site where nature rules. The silvery metal plays off the drought-resistant plantings that Vicki Myers has added to the sparse natural vegetation.

"When the fog clears, you think you are in Greece, looking down from the mountains to the changing tones of the ocean," says Myers. "But I'm just as happy lying in bed, looking back to the hillside, or out to the creek through a grove of live oaks. The house and studio open up on three sides so that the boundary between indoors and out disappears. I've always wanted a house that was integrated with the landscape, and this is it."

3 Floor plan of the main house
4 With the glass shutters raised, the living room becomes a portico
5 (overleaf) View of the house from across the pool atop the guest house

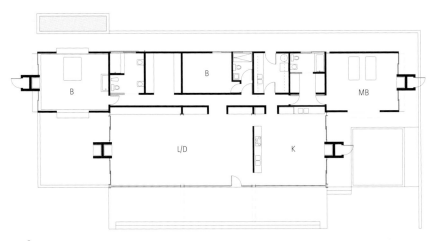

3

6 Roll-down steel shutters provide
security and fire protection
7 Drafting studio, with its wall of
books, at the top of the slope
8 Living room, looking down the
canyon towards the ocean

Howard and Judi Sadowsky bought a ranch house she describes as "hideous and broken down" for the sake of a tree in the back yard—a huge 300-year-old sycamore with a trunk that writhes like a prehistoric monster. It was love at first sight. A friend recommended "a brilliant young architect," and they invited Margaret Griffin, along with her partner John Enright, to transform the house. The goals were to strip the French country facade, break down internal divisions, open up to the lushly wooded site, and make the interior light and airy. It was to become a combination of stage and nest. Mr. Sadowsky heads a commercial brokerage firm, but he is also a passionate cook (last year he prepared an acclaimed six-course dinner for thirty to benefit the LA County Museum of Art) and he

craved a professional kitchen with lots of space for entertaining. "It had to work for me and make everyone else as comfortable as they would be in a conventional living room," he explains. They both wanted a congenial setting for their contemporary art, cozy spaces in which to relax by themselves, and guest rooms for their grown children.

The new 3,400-square-foot house grew organically out of the old, retaining its garage and the guest house above, staying close to its footprint, and utilizing a few of the outer walls and a part of the roof. The period-style facade has given place to a geometric abstraction, faced in steel-troweled gray stucco. The expansive living room to the right, an office and the master bathroom to the left are expressed as separate volumes, with translucent glass for privacy and

clear glass above. A projecting roof tilts up over the living room window like a raised eyebrow and hints at the most decisive change. In the old house, the gable roof was pulled down low, shutting out the sun even when it shone over the steep wall of the canyon. Griffin had the solution: flipping the lid. By cutting away the roof, tilting it up at front and back, and inserting skylights at the peak, the architects pulled in abundant natural light, late into the afternoon. They excavated the ceiling to reveal its hemlock boards and Douglas fir trusses, weaving these together with tie cords in the absence of a ridge beam and creating an undulating rhythm that echoes the canopy of branches. The front of the living room has been pushed out at an angle to accommodate a window seat; this gives

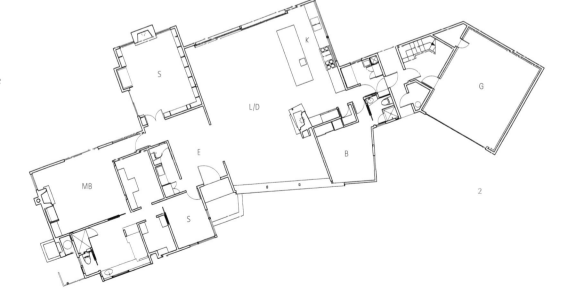

1 Uptilted roof and sleek facade
have transformed the old house
2 First floor plan

the roof a double tilt and addresses the curve of the street.

"The basic idea came quickly," says Griffin, "but we made increasingly large models to refine the junctions and other details. Each decision led us further. The scale was critical, whether you were standing or sitting. The design for the main space was fast-tracked in four months; other elements were designed during construction." Air-conditioning was built in but has never been used; and the clients find the two-zone system an economical way of heating the house.

The loftlike volume of the living area opens up through massive steel-framed sliders to the paved yard, which is often used for outdoor dining. Mahogany was selected for the floors to make the ceilings seem lighter—an

effect that is enhanced by uplights in the tie cords. Doors, window frames, and some of the cabinets are vertical-grain Douglas fir; the rest are birch. A fourteen-foot-long brushed stainless counter separates the kitchen from the dining table, and the owners have discovered that there is no need for a screen—noise and dirty dishes don't impinge on guests. Stacked, canti-levered granite slabs are used for the corner hearth and wraparound shelves, anchoring the room. "Howard favors contemporary, but I was afraid of a cold glass and steel box," says Mrs. Sadowsky. "Margaret gave it the warmth that made me feel comfortable."

Next door is a compact library with two cove-lit walls of books and a hearth surrounded with glass that replaces a solid wall and frames a part

of the sycamore. Mrs. Sadowsky is a writer and it's her favorite retreat. Beyond is the master bedroom with its high angled window, and the skylit, slate-floored bathroom, in which the cabinets and square mirrors seem to float against the translucent glass.

"We tried to create an environment that was original but easy to live in," says Mr. Sadowsky. "Most people get stuck with rooms they don't use, and crowd into an enclosed kitchen. We find that every part of the house works and—though the canyon can be dark—we never have to turn the lights on during the day."

3 A professional kitchen is inte-grated with the lofty living room
4 The dining area extends out through sliders onto the rear terrace

5 In the intimate library, walls of
books frame an ancient sycamore
6 Cabinets and square mirrors float
in light in the master bathroom
7 The sitting area beside the hearth
is lit from the sides and above

Many architects receive their first major commission from a member of their family, and few were better prepared for the job than David Chun, who had previously worked for Skidmore, Owings & Merrill, Richard Meier, and the design-build firm of Marmol & Radziner. Chun's father, who emigrated from Korea, asked him to design a multigenerational house in which, following Korean custom, he or his elder brother would live alongside their parents. "They were very involved in laying out the plan, and there were many discussions on how the house would be used, but they had faith in me and gave me a lot of creative room," he recalls. "I'm a modernist, but they weren't so keen and I had to win them over."

Chun was given a lot that was ninety feet wide and surrounded by mature trees. The house was to be 4,900 square feet, and he wanted to break up the mass and avoid the usual practice of plopping a large block in the middle of the lot and treating whatever space is left over as the yard. The architect decided to block out the landscaping—a Japanese garden with a koi pond and a waterfall, a dry garden, and a lawn—and weave the structure around it. He split the house into a two-story bedroom wing at the front, and a lofty, stepped living area to the rear, linked by a glazed sitting area and separated by an expansive deck that serves as an outdoor room for entertaining. That yielded an H-plan, in which one upright is aligned with the street and the other rotates up to twenty degrees to face the waterfall.

The street facade was treated like a wall, with the redwood-clad son's apartment resting atop a concrete base containing the master suite and a guest room. It shields the open, extensively glazed areas behind. "My parents were worried when the concrete was poured, and neighbors asked if we were building a bunker," Chun recalls. "They were reassured when the redwood cladding was added to the upper story." They were further soothed when the living wing was treated as a giant cabinet, with maple floors, cherry paneling, redwood soffits, and straight-grain Douglas fir doors and window shutters. The contractor, Minardos Construction, respected the simplicity of the design and achieved the refinement it required.

At the center of the impassive facade is a narrow opening, within

1 A spacious deck and glass-walled sitting room link the two wings
2 First floor plan

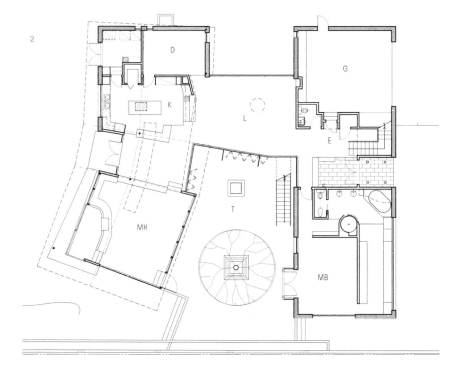

which a nine-foot-high stainless door pivots open and reveals the living spaces opening up on two sides through accordion doors to the redwood deck. It's a symbol of passage, from the public to the private realm, from opacity to transparency, and picks up on the practice, common to Asia and the Hispanic worlds, of entering a house through a door in the wall of a courtyard. Thus, a theatrical gesture, familiar to his parents, ties into a tradition that the Spanish brought to California. A steel stair leads up from the deck to the son's apartment and a railed gallery, complementing an indoor stair that leads out of the entry foyer. The sitting area opens south to the deck and looks north onto a Zen garden.

The kitchen, with its cherry cabinets and slate floor, is like a command post, stepping down to the breakfast room and the media room with its big-screen television. An open hearth with a stainless hood separates the media room from a little belvedere that opens onto a deck overlooking the water garden. The roof, supported on slender steel columns, extends out to shade this area from the setting sun. Though the furnishings are Western, the spirit is Asian: the space is an *engawa*, or raised in-between area from which to contemplate a stylized representation of nature and achieve a sense of peace. In contrast to this sequence of open spaces that blur the boundary between indoors and outdoors, the dining room is enclosed. The eucalyptus-toned walls and slate floors give it a sense of formality that sets it apart: a place for the family or close friends to come together as a tight-knit group.

The master bedroom has the same feeling of serenity and isolation with its platform bed, cherry paneling, a wall draped with a translucent fabric, Noguchi lamp, and low bentwood armchairs from Italy. Interior designer Jamie Bush made an intelligent choice of modern classics that include the M stool and Bruno Hansen's wooden dining chairs. However, furniture is sparingly used, emphasizing the floor in a tradition to which the client still feels attached.

3 Redwood cladding atop a poured concrete base on the street facade
4 An open hearth warms the media room with its low seating

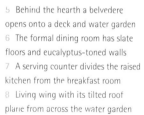

5 Behind the hearth a belvedere
opens onto a deck and water garden
6 The formal dining room has slate
floors and eucalyptus-toned walls
7 A serving counter divides the raised
kitchen from the breakfast room
8 Living wing with its tilted roof
plane from across the water garden

David Hertz is best known for compact, energy-efficient houses in Venice, but he has spread his wings over the past decade, designing a variety of buildings as far afield as Oregon. Keith Lehrer, formerly a drummer in a punk rock band and now CEO of his family's eyeglass business, saw an article on one of the early houses and picked Hertz to remodel a generic ranch house on a ridge high above Bel Air. He wanted a place of calm and order he could retreat to after stressful business trips, and he let the architect decide how to achieve this.

Lehrer wanted the work to proceed slowly, and that allowed Hertz to design for the site, responding to topography, views, prevailing breezes, and the orientation of sun, as he always prefers to do. Working closely with contractor Michael MacDowell, he remodeled the front of the house to serve as a temporary residence (and later as a guest wing) while the rest was leveled to make room for new construction. The Northridge earthquake cracked the original foundation, so that was replaced by a new steel structure rising from caissons. Existing trees were removed from the edge of the site where the ground drops sharply away, leaving a solitary pine that was sculpted by a Japanese gardener and revealing a vista of city lights and distant mountains. The pool to the rear of the house seems to flow into the reservoir far below. Dark green stucco makes the building recede into the landscape.

A spinal wall of steel-troweled black cement curves through the house, dividing public from private spaces, and extending from the entry to the master bedroom. At certain points it is cut away to become an arch or a balustrade, but its presence is always felt. Lehrer wanted an old-fashioned, wire-cage elevator with a staircase wrapped around it, leading up to a belvedere, and this was craned in as a pre-assembled, forty-foot-high unit of framed steel mesh. He also asked to see the lights of downtown from his bed, which is placed against the curved wall. To put him among the treetops, a balcony is cantilevered out towards two mature pines, saving their roots and shading a terrace. It is tapered and cut away at the end to open up the view.

The form of the living room was determined by tall pines on the opposite side of the house.

By putting the sitting area into a sunken pit, you have an unbroken view

1 Lofty living area, wire-cage elevator and second-floor master suite
2 First floor plan

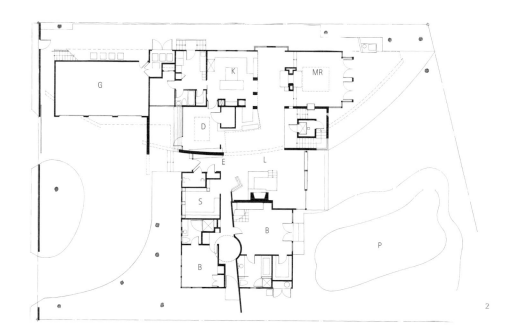

2

across the room to the horizon from the narrow rock crevice of the entry. The roof is high and tilted up so that, from the pit, you can see the full height of the pines outlined against the sky. Glass sliders open onto the lawn and pool. The white, steel-troweled plaster walls are a foil for the black concrete pit and spinal wall, the beech floor and built-in cabinets, and the exposed joists of recycled old-growth fir. Light floods or filters in from every side, blurring the divide between house and landscape, while three translucent glass columns pull light down into the recessed kitchen. Foliage casts its shadows on translucent glass in the master bathroom.

A Japanese influence is evident throughout the house, in the mono-chromatic palette, the openness to nature, the play of soft light and shadow, and the emphasis on the floor plane. The dining room looks into a walled Zen garden and has scrim-shaded ceiling lights. Hertz designed a slab table that can be raised or lowered hydraulically, allowing guests to sit on cushions or on Jacobsen chairs. The architect also designed the white cubist fireplace, which contains speakers, shelves, and amoebic figures in cut-out slots—an architectural sculpture that anchors the living loft. Kingsley, an LA artist, created a sonic sculpture on the curved wall of the upstairs gallery leading to the music room. It comprises eight strings, covering an octave, that can be plucked or bowed, which res-onate in the thick hollow floor and turn the house into a musical instrument.

"It's hard to call a 7,500-square-foot house 'green,' but it incorporates many environmental strategies," observes Hertz. "The elevator shaft works as a chimney with a shutter that opens automatically to evacuate hot air or recirculate it through the trusses of the second floor. We also have solar radiant heating and a high-efficiency mechanical system, and we specified non-ozone-depleting refrigerant, and zero voc paint in the master bedroom and other key interiors to reduce toxic emissions. Though high-efficiency glass costs more, the payback came quickly, and it allowed us to use a much higher ratio of glass to wall than in conven-tional buildings."

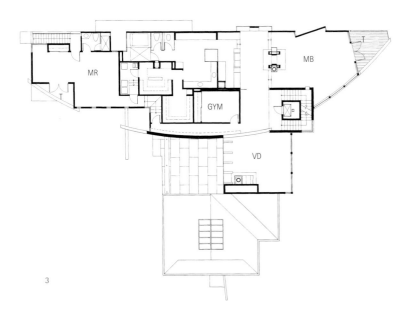

3

3 Second floor plan
4 Looking back from the seating pit in the living room to the entry

5 Translucent glass columns pull
light into the breakfast room
6 Play of shadow from skylight in
the steel-troweled stucco rotunda
7 The dining room hearth is as
sharply angled as a cubist sculpture

8 The curved spinal wall of black
cement is cut away in the gallery
9 The master bedroom balcony is
cantilevered into the treetops

Melinda Gray's heart beat faster as she heard the message on her answering machine: "I've bought a property in a canyon and want a cool Zen house, really minimal with concrete floors; give me a call back." The prospective client was Tom Schey, a peripatetic attorney with a teenage daughter, who explained that he had moved from the Midwest and wanted a place that opened up to the landscape and would give him "a rush of relaxation" when he came home.

"The existing house was pretty awful," Gray recalls, "a 1950s ski lodge with confined rooms, crummy wood-work and shag rug everywhere. I decided to break up the box, achieve a sense of connectedness within and outside, and make it more dynamic. The canyon provides a protective wall so you can be completely open on two sides without looking onto a neighbor. Tom gave me a free hand, though he was pretty involved at every stage, contributing ideas, and asking questions about colors and furniture. I'd show him several schemes and he'd always pick the best one."

She kept much of the two-story, 3,400-square-foot shell but carved into it, exposing the steel beams that were inserted to support open spans and reinforce the structure. The house was refaced with gray, steel-troweled stucco, and the pivoting glass doors and sliders on two sides of the living room were framed with straight-grain Douglas fir. These open up to a paved trapezoid patio with new boundary walls and a water feature. An outdoor hearth, a dining table, and wood chaises mounted on casters give the patio the character of an outdoor living room. From the path that zigzags to the upper garden, the house appears as a crisp, silvery form sitting lightly within the leafy canyon, its gray walls fading to invisi-bility beneath the new standing-seam Galvalume roof. The contractor, Jim Davis, did a great job.

Living spaces wrap around an open hearth and a new, wedge-shaped stair-case with a balustrade of wood posts and taut cables, and treads of com-pressed lumber (a material that is also used for the kitchen tabletop). The stair picks up on the angle of the hillside and the grid of the floor, where large brown-toned concrete tiles are aligned diagonally so that any cracks are more likely to occur in the grout. Fake antique ceiling beams were covered with plaster, and steel-lined channels

1 From above, the house is a silvery form engaging a leafy canyon
2 First and second floor plans

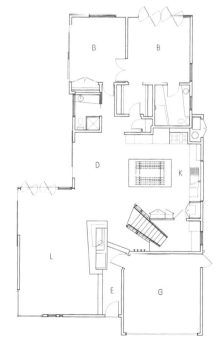
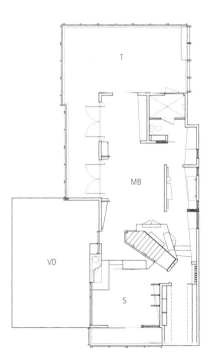

were cut into the smooth white surface to break up the expanse of the vault and conceal low-cost pin spots. These rhythmic slashes draw the eye up to the twenty-seven-foot-high pitch of the roof and the gallery that overlooks the skylit void around the staircase. The kitchen counter top was modeled of integrally colored precast concrete with a wave division between the two sinks, which have perforated metal inset into the bottoms. Understated contemporary furniture, including B&B Italia sofas, a glass-topped dining table, and an elegant oval sideboard, complement Gray's built-ins.

The second floor serves as a master suite, with an office at the front of the house. At the top of the stairs, there's a service concourse extending back from a walk-in closet, through a dressing area with open compartments for organizing clothes, to a glass mosaic-lined bathroom with a sculpted concrete sink, and a glass-screened shower from which you can step out onto a deck. In front of this long narrow space is the bedroom, which opens onto another side of the expansive new deck. From the bed, with its tilted storage wall that doubles as a headboard and swiveling plasma screen at the foot, you can look up through angled windows to the treetops and the pitch of the roof. Meticulously detailed built-in cabinetry explores the theme of opening and closing, with cut-outs in the doors and drawers replacing handles.

As in her previous, ground-up houses, Gray has demonstrated her mastery of space and detail, raw and refined, achieving a lively, playful character that never becomes too busy. For a client who professed a liking for warmth, hard lines, and a feeling of serenity, she has created a loft that works as well for him as it does for guests and parties—in which the boundary between indoors and out is obliterated. Above all, the house engages the canyon, carving out spaces at its base and providing many vantage points from which the wooded slope can be enjoyed. It's an elaborate treehouse—in contrast to the original, which was largely indifferent to the unique qualities of the site.

3 Angled steps lead up through a skylit void to the master suite
4 Entry gate set into the wall that encloses an outdoor living room

5 Gray designed the built-in cabinets with cutouts in place of pulls
6 In the master bedroom, the angled headboard contains storage
7 Above the sitting area, steel channels lead to the pitch of the roof
8 Compressed lumber is used for stair treads and kitchen counters

CONFINED LOTS

The American ideal remains a sprawling suburban house with expansive front and back yards, but, as cities become more populous and land costs escalate, people are buying smaller, better-located lots, and making a virtue of urban density. Here are five houses in which the constraints of narrow, busy, irregular, precipitous or built-up lots were a spur to creativity.

A gritty, 2,300-square-foot complex of three cubes, tightly sandwiched between neighboring properties, a street, and one of the Venice canals, is the inventive live/work space of Whitney Sander. One cube, housing a two-level studio, is raised on six-inch steel columns over the carport on the street front; two are stacked to form the house, which fronts the canal. They are separated by a pool and a spiral stair, enclosed by a metal grating, which leads up to the studio; their roof terraces are linked by a bridge. "We had to work within a twenty-two-foot-wide site, including three feet for the set-back entry and the side stairs that run down from the roof terrace," says Sander. "The narrowness made it tighter and more elegant. The two volumes play off each other and provide a

sequence of experiences you wouldn't get with one block." As you move from the utilitarian street to an idyllic water-front village, the complex becomes more permeable.

The entry to the house is tucked beneath the escape stair and is empha-sized by a bold accent of red cladding over the shear wall, a color Sander derived from a magnolia bud. Horizontal steel fins wrap around the south and west sides of the studio, shading its translucent Ciro plastic walls. A tall win-dow looking out to the street is shaded by a blind of brass mesh. Vertical steel louvers shade the house to the south, allowing a softly diffused light to filter in, and the last ten of these fan out to pull in ocean breezes. The cladding board to the north and east is protected by perforated metal, which catches the

light and reduces the bulk of the block. The house opens up to the canal through a wall of glass. An unfenced expanse of rounded pebbles deter cats and ducks from walking into the house when the door is open, and the sound they make warns off intruders like a nightingale floor—the creaking boards that protected a samurai from stealthy assassins in Edo-era Japan. Set in this stone garden are papyrus and two Noguchi-like rocks, one standing, the other reclining.

Within both volumes, surfaces have been folded, warped, and wrapped. The hard edges and orthogonal geometry of the house are softened by what Sander calls a "false Moebius strip" of sand-brushed acrylic that winds up around the central X-braced atrium to form a balustrade for the gallery, and a

1 Duplex studio over carport plays off the house fronting onto a canal
2 First and second floor plans

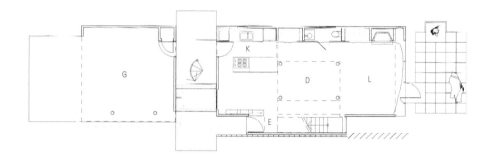

2

translucent screen around the bedroom and bathroom. The ground floor is divided into three zones. To the rear is a kitchen with an island of Wavecore Panelite (bubbled plastic) folded into an L-section. At the center is a dining area for which Sander designed the steel table base, and, at the front, inside the glass, is a sitting area furnished with heirloom pieces by George Nakashima that his parents bought the year he was born.

"The downside of having a glass wall a few feet from a public footpath is that everyone stops and looks in," remarks Sander, "and that prompted me to add parachute nylon drapes that can be drawn around the living area, providing privacy and an element of shade, in defiance of the prejudice most architects have against curtains." The

drapes soften the folded half-inch steel of the stair treads, fireplace, and mantel, and the steel columns that support the upper floor and the atrium with its double-glazed, gray-tinted skylight. The concrete floor has a glossy walnut stain. Upstairs, the surfaces are softer: a floor of bamboo steps up from the office to the master bedroom and folds up to form a parapet, from where you can look out over the canal without being seen from below.

For Sander, who launched his practice in 1987 after leaving Yale and the Peace Corps, and has focused his attention on innovative systems, this house is a laboratory for testing ideas and materials. Ruiz Brothers were the contractors and their skill allowed him to improvise during construction, although the basic configuration

remained unchanged. "The distinction between front/back, protected/open, work/live and space between was there from beginning," he observes. "I like the conceptual clarity and tried to layer the space and give it a tactile feel, with translucency, sinuousness, and varied textures. It is energy-efficient, with lots of openings for ventilation. Water circulates in the floor and the sun heats the space passively."

3 The house is set back from the canal path behind a stone garden
4 Vertical and horizontal louvers shade the studio and house

5 Steel columns form an aedicula
around the central skylit dining area
6 Brushed acrylic forms a balustrade
and screens bedroom and bathroom
7 A staircase of folded half-inch
steel plate is cantilevered from a wall
8 The bed is silhouetted against the
steel ribs and brushed acrylic

5

The house that architect Scott Johnson designed for his family breaks all the rules for Hancock Park—a tranquil enclave of huge trees and period-style homes in midtown LA. It is snugly inserted into a commercial, not a residential, street, and almost every foot of the site is used for building or parking. The pool is located on a second-floor terrace, and there is no leafy yard. Most arrestingly, the facade is wrapped in corrugated steel and glass curtain wall, with a semi-circular translucent glass lantern lighting the third-floor study. And yet, nobody has complained, and the house is as comfortable a fit with its neighbors as it would be in a tougher, more urban area.

"A lot of people wonder what this building is," says Johnson. "It doesn't have the signs and symbols that say 'house.' I live in LA, which is the story-telling capital of the world, but I don't believe in narrative architecture. It's a liberating experience to explore abstraction and solve problems without worrying about questions of image."

The challenge was to create a house that offers security and privacy, but opens up to views and the bustle of the street. Like the Japanese, who describe the view over a boundary wall as "borrowed landscape," the owners enjoy vistas of treetops and the Hollywood Hills, which make up for the lack of a garden. Johnson describes his creation as a "study in geometrical precision that is spacious enough for the four of us and allows for entertaining on any scale." He's constantly on the move, teaching and visiting far-flung job sites. His wife, Dr. Margaret Bates, runs a medical practice that can keep her up nights, and their teenage son and daughter wanted a soundproofed room for making music.

From the street, the shimmering cube is enigmatic; its 6,000-square-foot interior feels transparent and the spaces flow together. George Minardos did an exemplary job on the construction. An assertive steel staircase slices up through the center of the house, linking the ground-floor studio, service areas, and a spacious garage to the living areas on the second. The children's bedrooms are on the third and have expansive north-facing windows. In contrast, the second-floor master bedroom, separated from the living room by a pool terrace, is secluded and serene: a cylinder of ebonized wood and sound-absorbing fabric paneling with a sliding

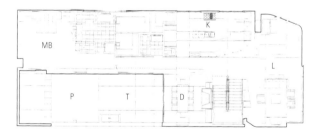

1 Corrugated steel-and-glass curtain wall wrap the street facade
2 First and second floor plans

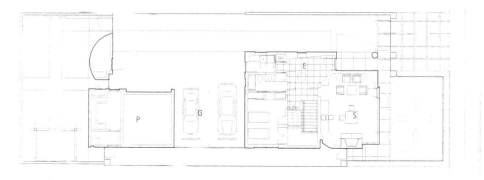

screen that blacks out the one narrow window. In a nod to Gordon Matta-Clark, a circle is cut through the ceiling to reveal the joists. It's an example of how Johnson has juxtaposed raw and refined materials throughout the house.

For a successful large-scale architect like Johnson, the design principal of Johnson Fain Partners who is best known for his sharply angled Fox tower in Century City, building a house is an indulgence—though it's one at which he has excelled. As a collector of contemporary art who also designs furniture, he wanted it to serve as a work in progress, a place to try fresh ideas and juggle the contents over a period of time. The polished concrete floors and lofty ceiling of the living room, the steel stairs and colored glass screen that divide it from the dining room, and

the translucent fiberglass that wraps the kitchen, all evoke an industrial loft. The living room, eclectically furnished with unfamiliar pieces and a grand piano, doubles as a music room. The dining room, with its elliptical tabletop of dark and creamy stone and its tall upholstered chairs, opens up through glass sliders to the pool terrace, turning it into a shady porch on summer days. A rusted steel beam in the cutaway ceiling plays off the elegance of the furnishings.

Having lived in New York's Greenwich Village and the Haight district of San Francisco, the Johnsons wanted to recapture the urban experience and share the fun of walking to neighborhood shops and restaurants. They find themselves at home in a village at the center of the metropolis, enjoying the

spectacle but shielded from noise. For Dr. Bates, who often has to catch up on her sleep after getting the kids off to school, it's ideal. "We are high enough up that it's very quiet," she says, "but the neighborhood is down to earth and it gave us a lot more freedom to express ourselves than if we had built on a typical residential street."

3 A steel-railed staircase slices through the loftlike living room
4 The dining room opens up to the second-floor pool terrace

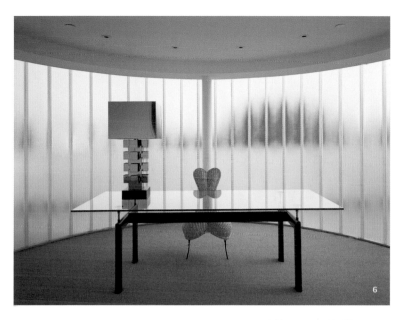

5 Johnson designed the elliptical table of dark and creamy stone

6 A semicircular bay of translucent glass lights the third-floor study

7 Circular plan of the master bedroom is echoed in ceiling cutout

Steven Kanner made his reputation in the architectural firm his late father established with a series of pop icons, notably a Googie-inspired In-N-Out Burger in Westwood Village, as well as some serious modernism. The 3,200-square-foot house he designed for his family in an unpretentious part of Pacific Palisades is a mix of whimsy and practicality, serious planning, and playful references. It is securely anchored to a hillside, but looks as though it is ready to sail away. The long white hull of scratch-coat stucco with its tilted prow, the portholes set into the detached stair tower that is faced in smooth blue mosaic, and the crossed steel cables that brace the structural frame, all evoke the ocean at the end of the street. The entry lobby, with its blue terrazzo floor and railed steps, suggests a ship's bridge. However, Kanner has made best use of a tight budget and a confined site to create a house that's full of light, fresh air, and joyful exuberance.

Cynthia Kanner, who heads post-production for HBO Films, loves the small-town feel of the neighborhood as do the couple's two young daughters. "The only reason to move from the house we had remodeled a few blocks away was the opportunity to build from scratch," says the architect, "and the site drove the design." It was sixty by 120 feet—the size of a professional tennis court—and the ground dropped sharply away. Neighboring houses were oriented to the street, blocking sunlight from their backyards. The Kanners decided to build along the north side, with three bedrooms extending back from the garage and living spaces tucked in below. That freed up the rest of the lot to serve as a sun-filled patio, and—thanks to expansive double-glazed windows—gave every room abundant natural light, even when the sea fog rolls in. Because the house is end-on to the street and steps down, it doesn't overwhelm the bungalows to either side.

The landscaping by Craig Doyle was a critical factor in creating a private world. Horizontally slatted cedar fencing is augmented by timber bamboo, black bamboo, and ficus hedging to screen neighboring houses, making it unnecessary to put blinds on the windows. In the front yard, a V-shaped palm sets off the facade, while bands of Japanese grass, gravel, and lawn amplify the scored pattern of the stucco.

The best place to enjoy the sensation of being indoors and out at the

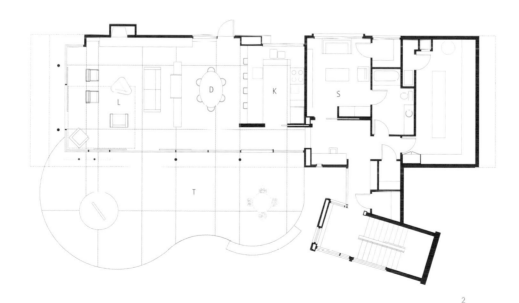

1 Double-glazed living room and stair tower flank a sun-filled patio
2 Lower floor plan

2

same time is the lofty living room, which opens up on two sides through glass sliders to a paved terrace and lawn. The easy flow of space within and out to Eric Orr's water sculpture makes the room seem much larger than it is, and the elegant modern furniture provides a sense of scale. There's a consistent use of inexpensive, hard-wearing materials: a polished concrete floor that catches the light, a wall of pale green mosaic that turns to yellow where it's lit from a concealed fluorescent strip, and a bookshelf unit of boldly grained fir plywood that floats on steel columns and is cut away to frame the dining area and open kitchen on the far side. Kanner has also made good use of corrugated fiberglass for garage and closet doors, clear-sealed medium-density fiberboard for storage units, and white

marble that proved almost as affordable as Formica for kitchen and bathroom counters.

Upstairs is as full of surprises and engaging details as down. Caroline, the elder daughter, got to choose the colors of her bathroom—silver mosaic "stars" on deep blue walls—and that of her baby sister, Charlotte. Their closets, splayed to accommodate storage trolleys, jut into the corridor leading to their parents' bedroom. This airy space overlooks the void above the living room which is sealed off by glass, creating the illusion that there is another room between this and the tilted glass wall at the west end of the house. The master bathroom is full of fun: large and small portholes with pivoting windows, and two overlaid circles of mirror glass that reflect the cylindrical shower.

The Kanners love their house and the neighbors clamor to see it, but the architect has decided that this is his farewell to pop. "I wouldn't design another house like this," he says. "It's time to move on." If he had any temptation to slide back, Caroline would rein him in. At age three, she produced an abstract collage dedicated to Frank Gehry with the inscription, "You are the best architect in the world."

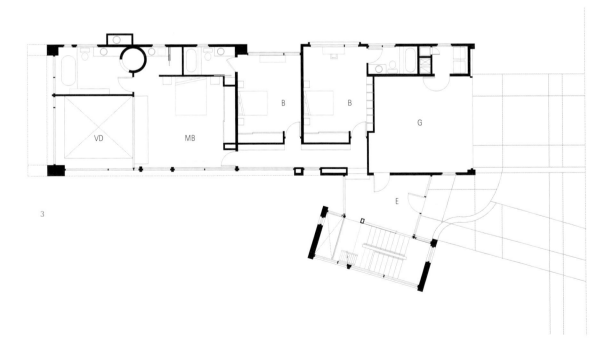

3

3 Upper floor plan
4 The double-height living room opens up to the south and west
5 (overleaf) Looking from the master bedroom/office to the living room

MARK ROTHKO

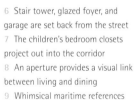

6 Stair tower, glazed foyer, and garage are set back from the street
7 The children's bedroom closets project out into the corridor
8 An aperture provides a visual link between living and dining
9 Whimsical maritime references evoke the ocean, a block away

In the 1930s, when land in LA was cheap and readily available, *Sunset* magazine gave away inaccessible plots as a premium to subscribers. Now, every piece of ground has its price and the hills are full of houses propped on stilts above cliff-faces. Lauren Lexton and Kevin MacCarthy, a young couple who moved to LA from New York, were drawn to Silver Lake, a neighborhood on the edge of downtown that inspired the first generation of modernists. "It was the vibe, the Macintosh-Beetle demographic," says MacCarthy, "and we loved the houses cascading off the hills, cheek-by-jowl, with great views." They searched and bought a site that rose at an eighty-degree angle from a winding street.

Scanning books in search of inspiration, they saw a house by Lorcan O'Herlihy but were hesitant to call him, supposing that an architect who built in Malibu would be too pricey. They soon discovered he had built all over the city and was as concerned as they to make every dollar count—notably in the house he is currently building for himself on a twenty-five-by-fifty-foot plot in Venice. MacCarthy is a storyboard artist who needs a home office, and Lexton is a documentary filmmaker, so a well-lit interior that required little maintenance was a must, along with space to entertain and two bedrooms.

The critical decision was where to position the house on the site. As O'Herlihy explains: "There is a thirty-six-foot height limit on hillsides but you can go to forty-five if the house is more than ten feet from garage; otherwise, to stay within the limit you would have to build straight up from the street. To place the house near the top of the site and meet code requirements, we had to shave the hill to reduce the average grade to forty-five degrees. Finally, since the retaining wall has to extend seven feet beyond the house, there was an incentive to keep it short and add a room upstairs." Nearly a third of the budget went to site preparation, the massive retaining wall, and twenty caissons that were driven into the bedrock.

The 2,000-square-foot house was shaped by the physical and financial constraints, which were turned to advantage. The approach is dramatic: a long flight of steps lead up the steep slope from the carport. In contrast to the generic boxes that are common in the hills, this has a two-story glass bay pushed up and slightly forward of the

1 The house, supported on caissons, projects from a steep hillside
2 First floor plan

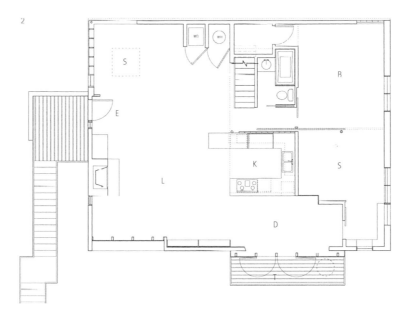

horizontal volume, both of which are wrapped by a lattice of pine boards over a watertight membrane. The house, which is cantilevered off a steel frame, had to be set fifteen feet forward of the retaining wall and this accommodates a level back yard and rear windows.

You enter at the side into an open living area, which is divided from the rear office by a silvery gauze curtain, and flows into the dining room. This is set up to the glass and opens onto a deck; the kitchen is enclosed by a counter. Two glazed slots allow light to filter in through the spaces between the exterior boards, and in the bay, the glass seems to slide past the inner white wall. Sliding doors of wood-framed translucent plastic separate a guest bedroom from MacCarthy's work space. Profilit,

a ribbed, molded glass, forms a translucent screen around the bathrooms on both levels. An open staircase leads up to the master suite, which occupies the upper half of the central bay. The bed juts from a sizzling orange wall, and you look out through a wall of glass to the city, a clerestory to the hillside, and a window on the other side where blue and white glass pebbles are arranged on the flat roof to suggest a pool.

"We never tire of view—it's the weather show, constantly changing," says Lexton. "The separation from the hillside gives us a great flow of space, and so much cross ventilation that we never need air conditioning, and require very little heating." MacCarthy praises the elegant simplicity of the two intersecting boxes, and the way every part of the house functions smoothly. Built-in

cabinets give a sense of depth and animate the interior.

"We kept costs down without compromising on quality by being inventive with materials," explains the architect. "The pine boards, bamboo floors, Douglas fir window frames, and the concrete board around the hearth were all very affordable, and I got a great deal on the Profilit. It's also a tribute to Ben Harrison of A+B Construction, that he wanted to solve problems and get it right."

3 The living area commands a sweeping view over midtown LA
4 An open staircase leads up to the master suite in the central bay

5 The dining area is set up to
the glass and opens onto a deck
6 Douglas-fir window frames
complement the pine-clad walls
7 The bathrooms are enclosed
with molded translucent glass

This house is a testimonial to the inventive, hands-on spirit of the Southern California Institute of Architecture in the way it exploits a corner site without overloading it, and uses a few basic materials to create a hierarchy of elegant, light-filled spaces. Geoffrey Kahn, Ken Mori, and Dane Twichell all graduated from SCI-Arc in 1990, and stayed in touch with each other. Kahn imports prefinished wood panel products from Europe and wanted an airy family house that would showcase these. He turned to Mori, who had worked for Arata Isozaki in Tokyo before setting up his design office in LA. "In Japan I lived in tiny, multi-purpose rooms and learned that bigger isn't better," recalls Mori, "and at SCI-Arc's campus in Ticino I got a taste of European rationalism. Here the goal was to achieve a physi-

cality through the meticulous detailing of simple materials. What makes the house special is what's not here."

Mori did schematic designs and then enlisted Twichell, who had worked for Frank Gehry before starting his own practice, to develop the design, using 3D software in lieu of models, and create the working drawings. In the absence of ornament, everything had to be precisely detailed, and the design process extended over eighteen months as a collaborative effort between client and architects. One contractor asked Kahn if he was trying to build a piece of furniture, but Jeff Wilson of Wilson Construction understood what was required and took pride in doing it exactly as the drawings specified.

Christina and Geoffrey Kahn have two young children, so they wanted

flexible living areas, but were willing to sacrifice extra space for a lofty void at the heart of the house, and a spacious backyard that separates the 2,750-square-foot house from the 900-square-foot garage-studio. Mori gave them a rectangular, wood-framed volume that is wrapped with a waterproof membrane, and clad with four-by-eight-foot sheets of Parklex 1000—a composite of resin-coated wood veneers with a bakelite core—spaced a half-inch apart to articulate the panels. These are attached with stainless steel fasteners to wood strips raised an inch above the membrane to allow air to circulate and avert the buildup of condensation from rain or sea fog. A minimally sloped roof plane projects out over the walls, and windows are arranged in abstract

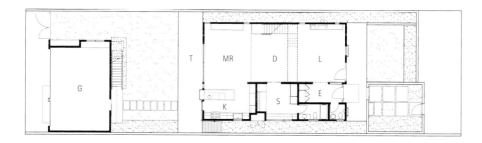

1 Stairs wrap around the dining area in the central skylit atrium

2 First and second floor plans

2

patterns, like the squares in a Mondrian painting.

Inside, three fifteen-foot bays contain the sitting, dining, and media areas in a single sweep of space that extends from a barn door in front to glass sliders that open onto the rear patio. Kitchen, bathrooms and a study are located in a semi-enclosed bar of space to the left, which concentrates the plumbing and mechanical services. The radiant-heated, ground-aggregate concrete floor was an inexpensive alternative to terrazzo, which would have been less durable besides looking too slick. An open steel staircase leads up through the twenty-six-foot-high, clerestory-lit atrium to the master suite and two children's bedrooms. Walls are paneled in different colors of FinPly screwed to drywall—yellow on the

service areas, natural in the dining area, green for the media room, and light brown in the master bedroom, which has a pale ash floor. Mori used the same material for his cabinetry and custom furniture, which includes a bright red coffee table, as well as for the stair treads, and window and door jams, integrating all these elements with the architecture.

What makes the house so remarkable is its warm minimalism, in which every element is pared down and precisely placed. The feeling is of a big cabinet with silky-smooth surfaces, perfect joints, openings, and projections that never clutter the simple lines. The geometric theme is announced in the forecourt with its low walls of poured concrete and square pavers, separated by bands of moss. The sheets of Parklex

establish a regular grid that unifies the two floors and the aluminum-framed windows cut into this. Two of the openings are layered with perforated metal (though Mori would have preferred to use acid-etched glass). Windows open on all four sides to pull in breezes from the ocean a half mile away, and the floor soaks up the warmth of the winter sun. A clerestory around the atrium pulls natural light into the center of the house, and opens to serve as a chimney that evacuates hot air. At night, uplights play off the galvanized aluminum ceiling intensifying the lighting behind the FinPly overlays and from the suspended paper lamp.

3 The house is clad with resin-coated panels of wood veneers
4 A barn door admits cool breezes and opens to the front yard

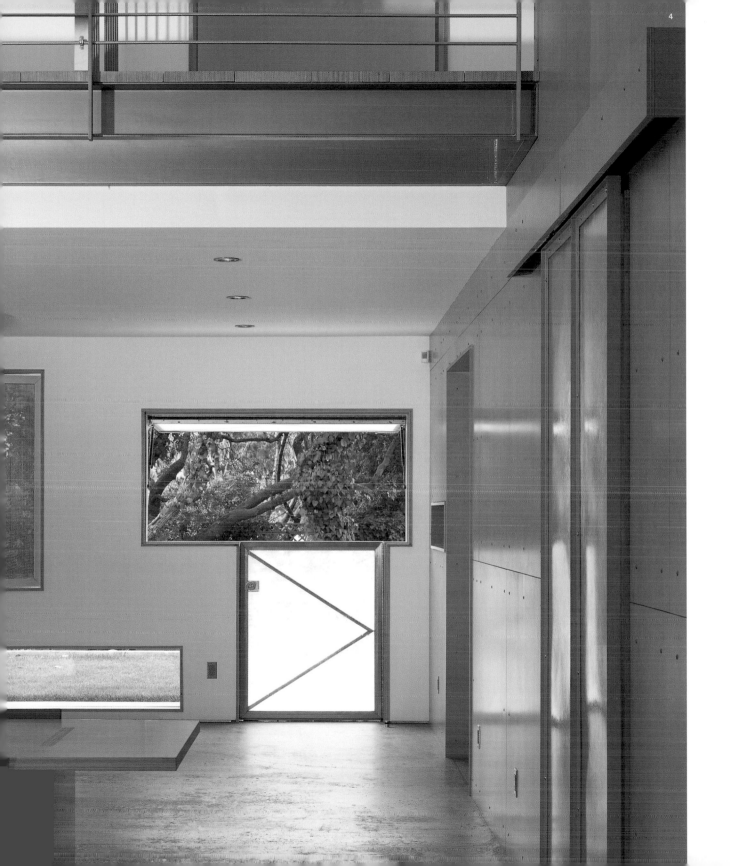

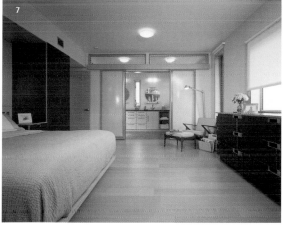

5 Sitting, dining, and media areas occupy a single sweep of space
6 A stair leads to the panel-clad studio atop the detached garage
7 The master bedroom has a pale ash floor and built-in cabinets
8 Concrete floors and FinPly assure warmth and practicality

RADICAL VISIONS

For many young architects, the computer serves as a tool used to develop ideas and test the feasibility of their designs, and it enables veterans to construct what they draw or model with no loss of spontaneity. A few visionaries use it to create fantastic structures that could be built for clients willing to abandon their preconceptions of what a house should be.

Pascal Brandys, a young French entrepreneur who specializes in genetic research, and his wife, Irena, divide their time between a Paris apartment and a modern house in Del Mar. To select an architect for his new residence, he flew his helicopter over San Diego County picking out the houses he liked, and gave the commission to Wallace Cunningham, the architect whose work impressed him the most.

Whirring helicopter blades inspired Cunningham and his associates to design a complex of linked pavilions that the client would view from the air, responding to the granite outcrops on a remote hilltop overlooking Lake Hodges. Three tapered steel columns support each of thirteen undulating triangular canopies that radiate like the petals of a flower or the folds of a dress. Each titanium-clad unit will be pre-assembled from metal deck spanning wave-shaped flange beams, and each will appear to float over its neighbor and the thirteen-acre site. Concrete floor pads linked by stairs step up and down the site and are cantilevered in places to preserve the natural slope. Low concrete walls define service areas at the core, and the perimeter is enclosed with mitered glass curtain walls, inclined at different angles, mounted on deep cushions at top and bottom, and braced with glass buttresses. Clerestory windows are set between the overlapping roof planes to pull light into the center of the house. The Ove Arup office in LA did engineering studies to ensure that the light, airy structure would withstand earthquakes and high winds.

As Cunningham observes: "The trick is to achieve the illusion of complexity with the simplest of means, and show what technology is capable of doing today. Next year, the parameters will have shifted."

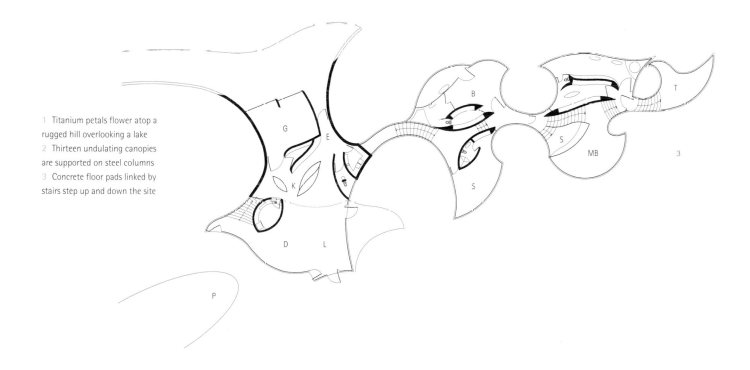

1 Titanium petals flower atop a rugged hill overlooking a lake
2 Thirteen undulating canopies are supported on steel columns
3 Concrete floor pads linked by stairs step up and down the site

1

2

3

Michael Maltzan worked for Frank Gehry as the project designer of Walt Disney Hall before setting up his own office and winning acclaim for MoMA's temporary home in Queens, N.Y., and Kid's Space in Pasadena. In both, torqued planes inflect space, and ramps thread through existing buildings to create a dialogue between old and new. He has used a similar strategy in a 4,000-square-foot house that was commissioned by Nick Scoville, director of astronomy at Cal Tech, and his wife, Zaha Turgel, a movie costume designer. Scoville had bought a 1940s bungalow, designed in Usonian style by Taliesin graduate Jim DeLong, in an enclave of classic modern houses with unfenced yards overlooking downtown LA. By lucky chance, he was able to acquire the two downhill lots on which to build

a larger house for himself, his new wife, and her son.

For Maltzan and project designer Yvonne Lau, the challenge was to engage the hill and the street, and to play off the bungalow, which will become a guesthouse. It's appropriate that a client who explores deep space through radio telescopes and enjoys sculpting should encourage his architect to create fluid forms. The lower-level wing of public spaces is placed at a forty-five-degree angle to the street as are the neighbors, and this is folded up and out to form an L-plan that extends back towards the bungalow. The house is anchored to the earth on the street side and dissolves into a glass-walled entry and stair hall on the inner face, leading up to the private rooms. The interplay of solid and trans-

parent, of shifting levels and layered geometries, makes this house a paradigm of the fire and energy to be found in the night sky.

1 A glass-walled staircase leads up from public to private rooms
2 Lower-level wing of public spaces is set at an angle to the street
3 Folded roof planes impart a dynamism to the house, inside and out
4 Axonometric of the two-level house

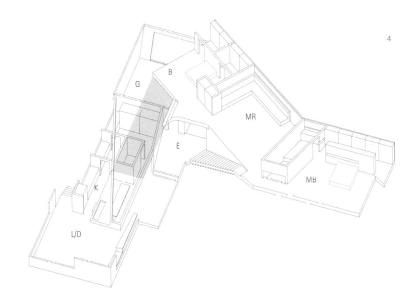

Thom Mayne heads an office that designs some of the most complex and exciting buildings in the world—on a scale that has grown from residential remodels to imposing schools, courthouses, and commercial developments. So he welcomed the opportunity to return to the scale and issues with which he began, and design a 3,000-square-foot house for his family. Three years ago, he began to explore the notion of prefabricating room-size units and placing them as a sequence of events within a loftlike volume of living space. He modeled a tilted block with trapezoid windows for a flat corner lot in Santa Monica, and the notoriously timid local authorities reacted as though they had come face-to-face with a Martian and nixed it. Unfazed, he and associates Ed Hatcher and Jean

Oei revised the design for a downhill lot. One linear block contains the carport, living spaces, and master suite; a second, separated from the first by a lap pool, is a bedroom wing for a guest and two teenage children. Both step down from a low street facade.

The architect invited Tom Farrage, a longtime collaborator, to fabricate a stainless steel carport and bathroom, a CorTen entry foyer, kitchen assembly, and wood bedroom in his metal shop. These will be lowered onto the site by helicopter, and the skylit, thirty-foot-high void of the living area will then be enclosed with an environmentally efficient skin. Windows will be shaped by the profile of each room, and floors will tilt up and down, imparting a dynamic rhythm to the interior. Fixtures and furnishings will be custom-designed,

giving each space a distinct but related character. Though the house may sound, from this description, to be a roller-coaster experience, the architects have planned a warm and woodsy bedroom, and intend that the kitchen remain the hub of family life.

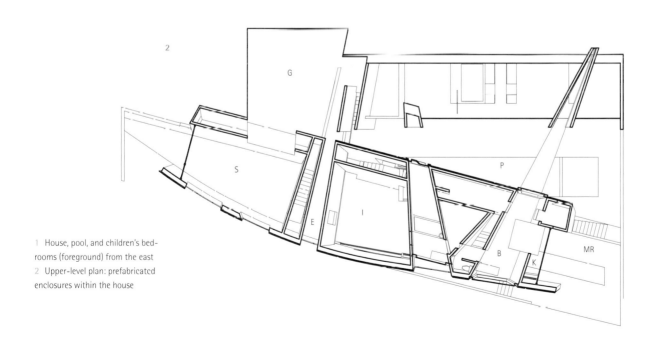

1 House, pool, and children's bedrooms (foreground) from the east
2 Upper-level plan: prefabricated enclosures within the house

3

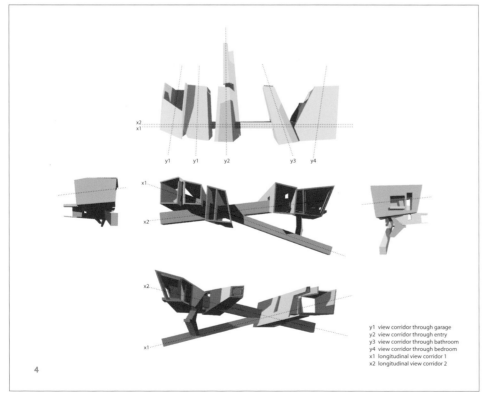

x2
x1

y1   y1   y2   y3   y4

x1

x2

x1

x2

x2

x1

4

3 House from south: windows are
shaped by the profile of each room
4 Views through each volume
contained within the outer shell
5 The house as the sum of its functions; each is separately expressed
6 From the entry foyer, you will be
able to look the length of the house
7 Longtitudinal section

y1 view corridor through garage
y2 view corridor through entry
y3 view corridor through bathroom
y4 view corridor through bedroom
x1 longitudinal view corridor 1
x2 longitudinal view corridor 2

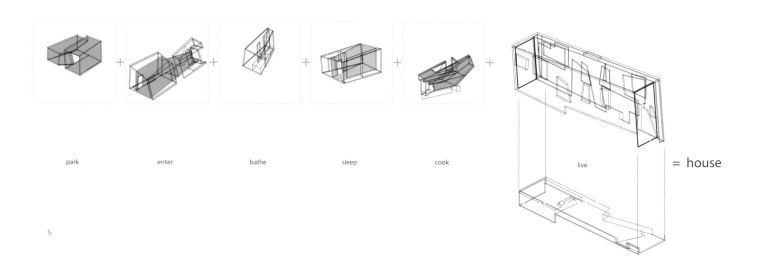

park   enter   bathe   sleep   cook   live   = house

5

6

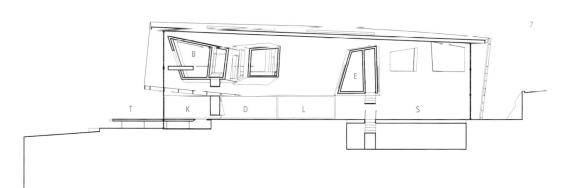

7

Fashion designer Leon Max had a dream that he was living in a cylindrical house and commissioned George Yu, the architect who designed an international chain of retail outlets for his company, to develop the idea. Yu left Morphosis in 1992 to establish an office that has won acclaim for innovative corporate spaces in America and Japan, and he responded with enthusiasm to this personal commission. Max imagined a romantic, ivy-clad turret that would be secure when he was traveling, but would open up to the landscape. The concept was fleshed out when the client found a gently sloping site high in the Malibu hills.

Over the past three years, Yu and his associate Sandra Levesque, have worked with Ove Arup to refine their design of an 8,000-square-foot house, partially enclosed by a circular concrete wall that will be half-buried in the hillside and faced, inside and out, by a thin layer of narrow limestone blocks. These pick up on the tone of rock outcrops, many of which will be cleared to provide a level pad. The wall is cut away to open the house to the south and a sweeping view of hills and ocean, with a projecting roof plane to shade windows from summer sun. A free-plan living room and design studio open through glass sliders to a circular patio with a demountable tensile awning, and a pool that extends the line of the outer wall. Walnut treads cantilevered from the stone-faced wall lead to the upper-level entry, sleeping areas, and gym. A drive descends from the guesthouse at the top of the slope to the entry, and continues down to a basement garage.

4

From above, the house appears as a solid monolith, from below as an open, airy pavilion.

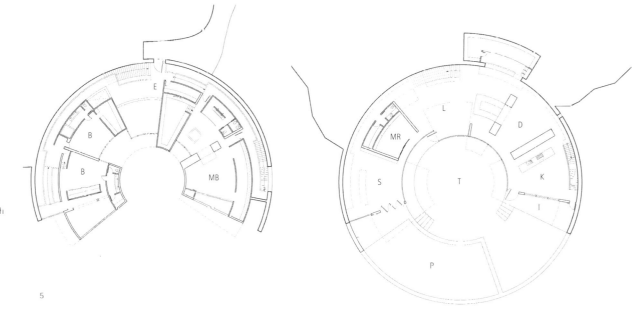

1 The house opens up to the south and a distant view of the ocean
2 An open-plan living area leads out through sliders to the patio
3 A circular, limestone-faced wall shields the house to the north
4 Ivy growing over the wall will merge it with the landscape
5 Upper and middle level plans

5

Cameron Crockett graduated from SCI-Arc and set up a computer design facility at Morphosis in the mid-1990s, before opening his own design-consulting office. He helped Daniel Libeskind, Rafael Moneo, and Michael Rotondi present their work, did illustrations, and won an AIA award for his own debut effort—a hypothetical, 7,000-square-foot house that is named for its computer file.

"The computer is incredibly liberating," says Crockett. "I developed this house as an exercise in three-dimensional sculpting, using Amorphium software and a pressure-sensitive pen to reconfigure an orthogonal volume. My first impulse was to create a beautiful form and dynamic volumes, but I added a level of rigor by inventing a site and a program, and giving it human scale.

It's something I could turn into working drawings and build."

If it ever is built, reports of UFO landings are likely to escalate sharply—as they did when Buckminster Fuller's Dymaxion house was erected on a farm in Kansas, a half century ago. In an overhead view of the rendering, the domed living area and tightly coiled service core seem destined to travel at warp speed, and the folds in the metallic skin might open to disgorge aliens. And yet, one can imagine an imaginative realtor giving a buyer a virtual tour of this dream house, with its sunken car port, forty-foot-high pleasure dome and sleeping gallery, lit from clerestories and light shafts. It's a twenty-first-century loft, an open plan, live/work space with few internal divisions, which could be minimally furnished and used

for parties. The more you consider the potential, the more likely it seems that some bold spirit will take up the challenge of living there. And if a willing contractor cannot be found, the teams that build movie sets as fantastic as this in a few days will be happy to pitch in.

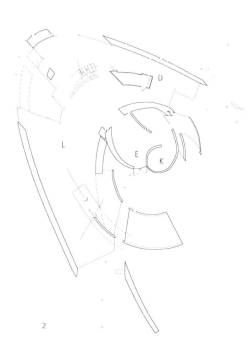

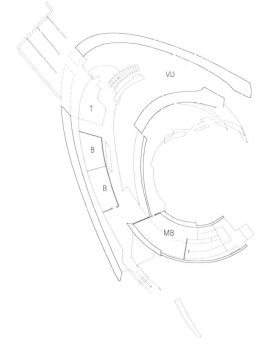

1 Stairs link the lofty living area to upper level bedrooms
2 Plans of lower and upper levels

3 A bar provides a transition
between entry and living area
4 Stairs linking the underground
parking to the upper level
5 View into the entry court, with
the living area to the left
6 Aerial view of the house from a
hovering mother ship

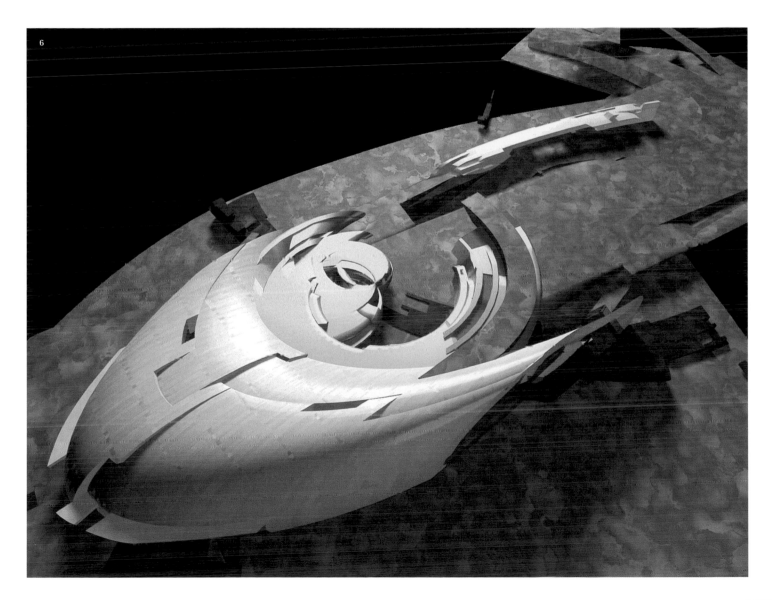

6

FEATURED ARCHITECTS

Stan Allen
609 258 3737
stallen@princeton.edu

BAM Construction/Design
310 459 0955
brianm@bamcdi.com

Hagy Belzberg
310 453 9611
hagy@belzbergarchitect.com

Callas Shortridge
310 280 0404
barbara@callas-shortridge.com

David Chun
310 314 1817
david@chunstudio.com

Cameron Crockett, Keleide Studio
714 542 1220
cameron@keleide.com

Wallace Cunningham
619 293 7640
wally@wallacecunningham.com

Alice Fung & Michael Blatt
323 255 8368
fungblat@flash.net

Ron Godfredsen & Danna Sigal
310 664 0302
danna@godfredsensigal.com

Melinda Gray
310 454 7960
melinda@graymatterarchitecture.com

Margaret Griffin & John Enright
310 391 4484
mgriffin@griffenenrightarchitects.com

Gwathmey Siegel
212 947 1240
info@Gwathmey-Siegel.com

David Hertz, Syndesis
310 829 9932
hertzaia@syndesisinc.com

Michael Jantzen
661 513 9901
mjantzen@yahoo.com
www.humanshelter.org

Scott Johnson, Johnson Fain Partners
213 622 3500
info@johnsonfain.com

Steven Kanner, Kanner Associates
310 208 0028
kanner@kannerarch.com

Finn Kappe
310 455 9720
fkappe@aol.com
www.fkappestudio.com

Ray Kappe
310 459 7791
rkappe@flash.net

Michael Maltzan
323 913 3098
mmaltzan@mmaltzan.com

Thom Mayne, Morphosis
310 453 2247
studio@morphosis.net

Moore Ruble Yudell
310 450 1400
info@mryarchitects.com
www.MooreRubleYudell.com

Ken Mori
310 208 1045
k.mori@verizon.net

Barton Myers
310 208 2227
mail@bartonmyers.com

Neumann, Mendro &
Andrulaitis Architects
805 684 8885
rincona@aol.com

Edward R. Niles
310 457 3602

Dean Nota
310 374 5535
dean@dnala.net

Lorcan O'Herlihy
310 398 0394
loh@loharchitects.com

Michael Palladino
Richard Meier & Partners
310 208 6464
palladino@rmpla.com

RoTo
323 226 1112
roto@rotoark.com

Whitney Sander
310 822 0300
wsarch@earthlink.net

Holger Schubert
310 287 1876
has@archisis.com

Patrick Tighe
310 450 8823
patrick@tighearchitecture.com

Dane Twichell
310 836 3223
twicstudio@aol.com

George Yu
310 313 4775
george@georgeyuarchitects.com

ACKNOWLEDGEMENTS

My deep appreciation to the owners of these houses for their warm hospitality and their generosity in agreeing to be included. It was a pleasure to feature work by some of my favorite architects, and I hope that the houses shown here will bring them many more commissions. I regret that I was unable to include anything by Daly Genik, Steven Ehrlich, Frederick Fisher, Glen Irani, Koning Eizenberg, Mark Mack, Eric Owen Moss, Rob Quigley, and, of course, Frank Gehry, who have done so much to enrich the architectural legacy of Southern California. Important new houses are not always ready in time for a publisher's deadline. I would like to salute the brilliant photographers whose images bring this book to life, and thank Grey Crawford, Erhard Pfeiffer, Tim Street-Porter and Michael Weschler for taking new shots. I'm indebted to Charles Miers of Rizzoli-Universe for commissioning this book and to my devoted editor, Steve Case, for guiding it to completion. Joseph Cho and Stefanie Lew of Binocular, did a superb job of design, as they did on my last book for Universe. Friends pitched in with valuable recommendations and ideas. Thanks to Christine Anderson, Frances Anderton, Kate Ayrton, Laura Hull, Merry Norris, Barbara Thornburg, and most of all to Jenny Okun and Richard Sparks for their inspired choice of title.

PHOTO CREDITS

Assassi Production 115
Tom Bonner 176, 179–181
Benny Chan Fotoworks 74, 78, 79 (7 & 8), 114, 116
Grey Crawford 182, 184–187
John Ellis 77, 208 (6 & 8), 209
Scott Frances 54–56, 58–60, 62–65
Scott Frances/Esto Photographics 66, 69–73
Art Gray front cover, 36–41, 164, 166–169
Douglas Hill 210, 212–215
Kenneth Johansson 86–88, 90–91
John Edward Linden 205–207, 208 (7), 216, 218–221
Grant Mudford 156, 159–163
Erhard Pfeiffer 28–35, 42, 44–47, 80, 82–85, 142, 144–147, 196, 198–201
Sharon Risedorph 188–190, 192–195
Tim Street-Porter 2–3, 14, 16–20, 22–27, 76, 79 (6), 92, 95–98, 100–103, 110, 112–113, 117, 154–155, 170, 172–175, 202
Michael Weschler 104, 106–109, 118–120, 122–125, 134, 137–141
Bill Zeldis 148, 150–153
Atelier Kim Zwarts 12, 48–53, 126, 128, 130–133